GCSE OCR Additional Applied Science Revision Guide

This book is for anyone doing **GCSE OCR Additional Applied Science**.

Applied Science is all about **experiencing science**.
But more than that — it means **understanding** the role of scientists in the real world by actually **doing the science yourself**.

And you can't do that without a fair chunk of **background knowledge**. Hmm, tricky.

Happily this CGP book includes all the **science facts** you need to learn, and shows you how they work in the **real world**. Not only that, we've given you loads of **handy advice** for doing **practicals** and getting stuck into those **reports**. And in true CGP style, we've explained it all as **clearly and concisely** as possible.

It's also got some daft bits in to try and make the whole experience at least vaguely entertaining for you.

What CGP is all about

Our sole aim here at CGP is to produce the highest quality books — carefully written, immaculately presented and dangerously close to being funny.

Then we work our socks off to get them out to you — at the cheapest possible prices.

Contents

Unit 1: Topic 1 — Sport and Fitness

Fitness Facilities	1
Baseline Assessment	2
Basic Tests	3
More Basic Tests	4
The Breathing System	5
The Blood and Blood Vessels	6
The Heart and Respiration	7
The Kidneys	8
Joints	9
Monitoring and Improving Performance	10
Physiotherapists	11
Fitness Practitioners — Good Practice	12
Revision Summary	13

Unit 1: Topic 2 — Health Care

Organisations Involved in Health Care	14
People Involved in Health Care	15
Public Health	16
Medical History	17
Prioritising Treatment and Resources	18
Treatment	19
Pregnancy	20
IVF	21
Antenatal Care	22
Blood Tests	23
Post-Natal Care	24
Revision Summary	25

Unit 1: Topic 3 — Protecting the Environment

Scientists and Environmental Protection	26
Good Laboratory Practice	27
Taking Samples	28
Visual Examination	29
Types of Testing	30
Testing Water Quality	31
Revision Summary	32

Unit 1: Topic 4 — Protecting the Public

Scientists Protecting the Public	33
Colorimetry	34
Chromatography	35
Microscopes	36
Interpreting Images from Microscopes	37
More on Visual Examination	38
Electrophoresis	39
Revision Summary	40

Unit 2: Topic 1 — Sports Equipment

Designing Sports Equipment	41
Mechanical Properties	42
Force-Extension Graphs	43
Thermal Properties	44
Material Properties	45
More on Material Properties	46
Revision Summary	47

Unit 2: Topic 2 — Stage and Screen

Managing Stage and Screen 48
Managing Light 49
Optical Properties 50
Lenses 51
Lenses and Images 52
Acoustic Properties 53
Controlling Sound 54
Managing Sound and Electrics 55
Managing Indoor Venues 56
Revision Summary 57

Unit 2: Topic 3 — Agriculture and Biotechnology

Agriculture in the UK 58
Regulating Agriculture and Food 59
More on Regulating Agriculture and Food 60
Organic and Inorganic Farming of Wheat 61
Wheat Production 62
More on Wheat Production 63
Rearing Cattle For Milk 64
Breeding Cattle 65
Processing Milk 66
Microorganisms — Uses and Dangers 67
Products From Microorganisms 68
More Products From Microorganisms 69
Growth of Microorganisms 70
Bioreactor Conditions 71
Genetically Modified Microorganisms 72
Revision Summary 73

Unit 2: Topic 4 — Making Chemical Products

The Chemical Industry 74
Regulating the Chemical Industry 75
Risk Assessments and Hazchem Symbols 76
Industrial Production of Chemicals 77
Acids and Alkalis 78
Reactions of Acids 79
Reactions of Acids and Chemical Formulae 80
Solutions 81
Making Insoluble Salts 82
Making Soluble Salts 84
Neutralising an Acid 85
Chemical Synthesis and Yields 86
Rates of Reaction 87
Mixtures 89
Testing Formulations 90
Revision Summary 91

Unit 3 — Controlled Assessment

Standard Procedures 92
Suitability Tests 94
Work-related Report 98
Report Writing Advice 102

The Perfect Cup of Tea 103
Index 104
Answers 108

Published by CGP

From original material by Richard Parsons.

Editors:
Charlotte Burrows, Helena Hayes, Rosie McCurrie, Rachael Rogers, Hayley Thompson.

Contributors:
Mark A. Edwards, Philip Rushworth, Sophie Watkins and Chris Workman.

ISBN: 978 1 84762 881 7

With thanks to Janet Cruse-Sawyer and Jamie Sinclair for the proofreading.
With thanks to Anna Lupton for the copyright research.

With thanks to Science Photo Library for permission to reproduce the photographs on pages 36 and 37.

With thanks to BSI for permission to reproduce the Kitemark symbol on page 41.
Kitemark and the Kitemark symbol are registered trademarks of BSI.
For more information visit www.kitemark.com

With thanks to Defra for permission to reproduce the crop data on page 58.

With thanks to the Health Protection Agency (HPA) for permission to reproduce the foodbourne outbreaks data on page 67.

Pages 76 and 91 contain public sector information published by the Health and Safety Executive and licensed under the Open Government Licence v1.0.
http://www.nationalarchives.gov.uk/doc/open-government-licence/

Groovy website: www.cgpbooks.co.uk

Printed by Elanders Ltd, Newcastle upon Tyne.
Jolly bits of clipart from CorelDRAW®

Photocopying — it's dull, grey and sometimes a bit naughty. Luckily, it's dead cheap, easy and quick to order more copies of this book from CGP — just call us on 0870 750 1242. Phew!

Text, design, layout and original illustrations © Coordination Group Publications Ltd. (CGP) 2012
All rights reserved.

Unit 1: Topic 1 — Sport and Fitness

Fitness Facilities

Hello, good evening and welcome to OCR Additional Applied Science. Now, if you want to be any good at this applied lark you'll need to be on top form — mentally and physically. So what better way to start than with a whole section on everyone and everything involved in keeping you fit.

Local Organisations Provide Fitness Facilities

People exercise at local fitness facilities, like leisure clubs and football clubs. Some of these facilities are provided by local authorities (paid for by taxes) but others are privately run (everything is paid for by the members). These fitness facilities provide a range of different services, for example:

LEISURE CLUBS provide...
1) Fitness equipment — e.g. weights and cardiovascular machines.
2) Personal trainers — devise a fitness plan for clients to follow and help motivate them (see below).
3) Fitness classes — e.g. aerobics or yoga provide different ways of working out.

FOOTBALL CLUBS provide...
1) Training sessions — players practise their football skills and do exercises to keep fit.
2) Coaches — work with a team of players to help them play better football (see below).
3) Matches — players compete in teams to win games.

Having fitness facilities nearby means people may be more likely to exercise regularly, which has lots of health benefits, e.g. losing weight, lowering blood pressure, getting rid of stress. Regular exercise can also be important in rehabilitation after illness or injury — e.g. patients who are recovering from surgery. Leisure and sports clubs also provide jobs and social events for local people.

Coaches and Personal Trainers Work at Fitness Facilities...

A coach generally works with a group of people to make them better at a specific sport or skill. A personal trainer usually works with an individual to improve their fitness. The types of scientific and technical skills that coaches and personal trainers need to do their jobs are similar, for example:

1) They must be able to carry out basic tests to assess a person's fitness (see pages 3-4).
2) They must understand how the human body works (see pages 5-9).
3) They must be able to develop and modify a fitness programme — a set of recommendations about the amount and type of exercise the client should do, how to exercise effectively, and diet.
4) They must be able to monitor a person's fitness (see p.10).

Coaches and personal trainers working at fitness facilities may have a sports science qualification. This shows they have the right skills for the job, and understand health and safety (see below).

...and Must Follow Health and Safety Regulations

By law, coaches and personal trainers must follow regulations (rules) to help keep themselves and the people they work with safe and well. These Health and Safety Regulations affect their day-to-day job, for example:

1) They must check that any fitness equipment is safe to use, to prevent injuries.
2) They must be able to show clients how to carry out exercises correctly, to prevent injuries.
3) They might need a first aid qualification to be able to treat any injuries that occur.

For your own health & safety in the exam...

... you need to know this page really well. That means you need to learn the two examples of fitness facilities (leisure and football clubs) and the services they provide. You also need to know what coaches and personal trainers do and the similar skills they have. Then you can give your brain a well-needed rest from its workout...

Unit 1: Topic 1 — Sport and Fitness

Baseline Assessment

Before a coach or fitness instructor can make up a fitness programme for a new client, they need to find out more about that person's initial (starting) fitness. This means they can make a programme that matches a client's needs and is safe, e.g. if a fitness programme is too hard for a client they may become ill or injured.

Clients are Asked Questions on their Lifestyle, Health and Fitness

Finding out about a person's initial fitness is called a baseline assessment. As part of a baseline assessment, a coach or fitness instructor may ask a new client questions on the following things:

LIFESTYLE
1) This is the way a person lives their life.
2) It includes what food a person eats, how much alcohol they drink, how many cigarettes they smoke, the amount of exercise they do and how much stress they're under. For example, if a person says they smoke 10 cigarettes a day they are talking about part of their lifestyle.

HEALTH
1) Health is a state of complete mental, physical and social well-being. It also means being free of any infections or diseases.
2) A person's health may relate to any medicines they are taking (e.g. antibiotics) and any previous treatments they have had (e.g. operations).
3) Health also relates to someone's personal history, e.g. if they've been or are pregnant, what previous injuries they've had. So, if a person says they sprained their ankle last year they are talking about their health.

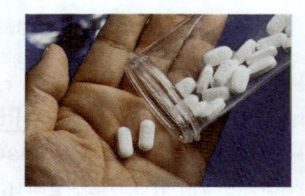

FITNESS
1) Fitness is a measure of how well you can perform physical tasks.
2) It includes the following things:
   - Aerobic fitness — the ability to exercise your whole body for a long period of time. (This is also called stamina.)
   - Strength — the amount of force that a muscle can apply.

Derek's stamina was low — his arm felt heavy after three swigs of tea.

You Need to Know How Lifestyle Factors Affect Fitness

The following lifestyle factors can have a negative effect on your fitness:
1) Food — a balanced diet is a diet that contains the right amount of all the nutrients you need. If you don't eat a balanced diet (e.g. if you don't eat enough carbohydrates or fats) you may be unable to perform certain physical tasks.
2) Drink — if you don't drink enough water you might not be able to perform certain physical tasks. Drinking too much alcohol can also affect your fitness, e.g. it slows your reactions, it makes your muscles get tired more quickly.
3) Amount of exercise — too little exercise means your muscles and bones will be weaker, and you'll have less stamina. This means you may be unable to perform certain physical tasks or may be more prone to injury if you do.
4) Stress — when you get stressed you get more emotional. Getting too emotional can make you tense, anxious or aggressive — making it harder to concentrate and perform physical tasks.

My stamina is great — I can sit through loads of re-runs of One Tree Hill...

Remember — lifestyle is the way you live, health is a state of complete mental, physical and social well-being, and fitness is how well you can do physical tasks. I'm not joking when I say you need to know what these three things mean for the exam. Once you've learnt this you can treat yourself — back to One Tree Hill maybe...

Unit 1: Topic 1 — Sport and Fitness

Basic Tests

After you've been quizzed, the next part of a baseline assessment involves taking a number of basic measurements such as height, pulse rate, body temperature and blood pressure.

A Baseline Assessment Will Involve Basic Tests Like...

...Recording Simple Statistics Like Age, Gender & Height

1) These might seem like pretty irrelevant facts for a coach or personal trainer to need to know, but they're actually quite important. For example, pulse rate (a measure of your heart rate) and blood pressure can be affected by age.
2) Height is important when calculating things like body mass index (see next page).

...Taking Your Pulse Rate

Here's how it's normally done:

1) The first and second fingers are placed on the artery on the underside of the wrist.
2) Using a stopwatch, the number of pulses in sixty seconds are counted.

A healthy adult pulse rate is 60-100 beats per minute at rest. A pulse rate outside this range might mean that the person has a health problem.
E.g. a high pulse rate might mean that the person has a heart disorder.

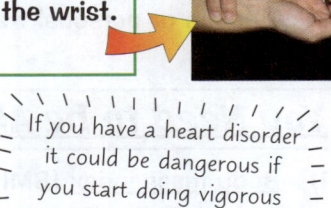

If you have a heart disorder it could be dangerous if you start doing vigorous (hard) exercise.

...Measuring Body Temperature Using a Thermometer

There are various types of thermometer that can be used to record body temperature:

1) A clinical thermometer — a bog standard thermometer that you stick under your armpit or tongue.
2) An electronic digital thermometer — a fancy thermometer that you put in your ear — it gives a digital reading.
3) A liquid crystal thermometer — a plastic strip that's placed on the skin (usually on the forehead) and changes colour to show the temperature.

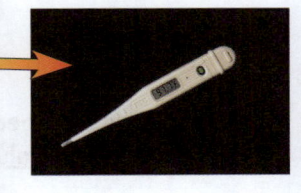

Normal core body temperature is 36.5 - 37 °C. A body temperature outside this range might mean that a person has a health problem. E.g. a high temperature might be a sign of an infection.

...Measuring Blood Pressure With a Sphygmomanometer

1) A sphygmomanometer is made up of an inflatable cuff that goes around your arm, and a pressure monitor. Blood pressure is determined using a stethoscope.
2) You can also get ones with electronic sensors that do it all automatically.

Normal blood pressure is about 120/80 mmHg. A blood pressure reading outside this range might mean that the person has a health problem. E.g. a high reading means the person has high blood pressure, which could lead to heart disease.

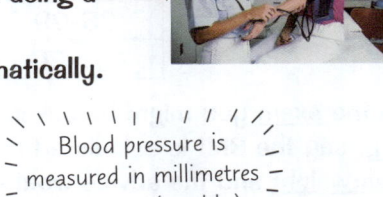

Blood pressure is measured in millimetres of mercury (mmHg).

I can spell sphygmomanometer — what's my prize...

You might be given a person's test result (e.g. for blood pressure) and the normal range for it. Then you might be asked what the result means — to do this compare the test result to the normal range and say whether it is within the normal range, too high or too low. A result outside the normal range might show a health problem.

Unit 1: Topic 1 — Sport and Fitness

More Basic Tests

There are two more basic tests that a personal trainer or coach might carry out as part of a baseline assessment. These tests measure your aerobic fitness and something called your body mass index. Guess what — you need to know all about them...

Basic Tests Include Measuring Aerobic Fitness Too

1) Aerobic fitness (see p.2) is another important health indicator.
2) One way to measure aerobic fitness is to carry out a step test. This basically involves:

   - Stepping up and down on a step for five minutes.
   - Measuring the pulse rate at one, two and three minutes after stopping.
   - Using a formula to calculate the step test score.

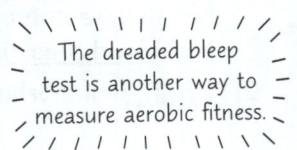

   The dreaded bleep test is another way to measure aerobic fitness.

3) The step test is a way of measuring your recovery rate — the length of time it takes for your heart rate to return to normal after exercise. The fitter you are, the faster your heart rate falls.
4) The result of a step test will show whether you have poor, average or good fitness for your age and sex.
5) A coach or personal trainer can use this result to make up a fitness programme that's right for you.

You Need to be Able to Calculate Body Mass Index

1) Body mass index (BMI) tells you whether a person's body weight is below, above or within the normal range.
2) A person's height is measured using a tape measure and their weight on some weighing scales.
3) Their BMI is calculated using the formula on the right.

   E.g. Steve is 1.8 metres tall and weighs 105 kg.

   Steve's BMI = $\frac{\text{body mass}}{(\text{height})^2}$ = $\frac{105}{(1.8)^2}$ = $\frac{105}{3.24}$ = 32.4

   $$BMI = \frac{\text{body mass}}{(\text{height})^2}$$ (kg) (m)

   You'll be given this equation in the exam — make sure you can use it.

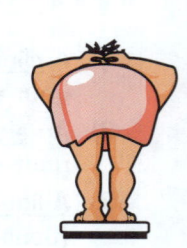

4) The coach or personal trainer can then compare the result to values in a table (see below.)

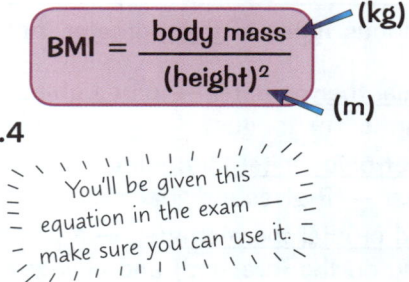

A Normal Body Mass Index is 18.5-24.9

1) Once a person's BMI has been calculated the results are interpreted using a table like the one below.

BMI	Condition	Advice
<18.5	underweight	gain weight
18.5-24.9	healthy weight	-
25-29.9	overweight	weight loss advisable
>30	obese	need to lose weight

2) In the exam you might be asked to calculate BMI then interpret the results. It's pretty easy — e.g. say the BMI is calculated as 27.5. This falls between 25-29 so the person's condition is overweight and the advice would probably be to lose weight.
3) You won't be given a table like the one above in the exam, so you need to learn it.

Let's work out your BMI baby...

The BMI equation might look a bit tricky but working through an example like the one above will make it clearer. In the exam, you might be given a person's BMI and asked to say what it means — so make sure you know what the BMI is for being underweight (<18.5), healthy weight (18.5-24.9), overweight (25-29.9) and obese (>30).

Unit 1: Topic 1 — Sport and Fitness

The Breathing System

As part of a baseline assessment (see p.2) coaches and personal trainers need to assess a person's health. To do this they need to understand all about how the human body works...

The Breathing System is in the Top Part of Your Body

There are a few parts you need to know...

1) The lungs are the organs where gas exchange happens — oxygen goes into the blood and carbon dioxide moves out.
2) The trachea (the pipe connecting your mouth and nose to your lungs) splits into two tubes called 'bronchi' — one goes to each lung.
3) The bronchi split into progressively smaller tubes called bronchioles and end with small sacs called alveoli — this is where gas exchange occurs (see below).
4) The ribs protect the lungs and the heart etc. They're also important in breathing (see below).
5) The intercostal muscles are the muscles in between the ribs.
6) The diaphragm is the large muscle at the bottom of the lungs, which is also important for breathing.

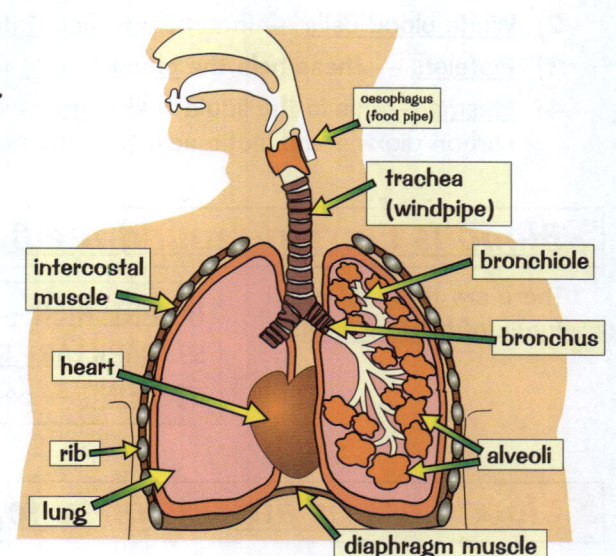

Alveoli have special features, for example:
- They have thin walls.   • They have a large surface area.

Both of these features help to speed up gas exchange.

Breathing In and Out Uses Muscles

The diaphragm and intercostal muscles play an important role in breathing in (inhaling) and out (exhaling).

Breathing In...

1) The intercostal muscles and diaphragm contract.
2) The ribcage moves up and out.
3) The lung volume increases.
4) This draws air in.

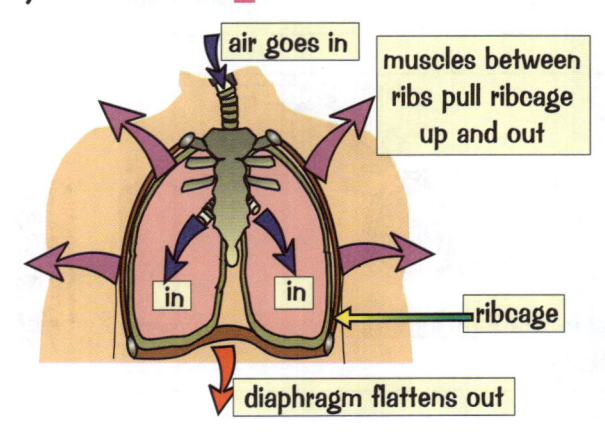

...and Breathing Out

1) The intercostal muscles and diaphragm relax.
2) The ribcage drops down and in.
3) The lung volume decreases.
4) Air is forced out.

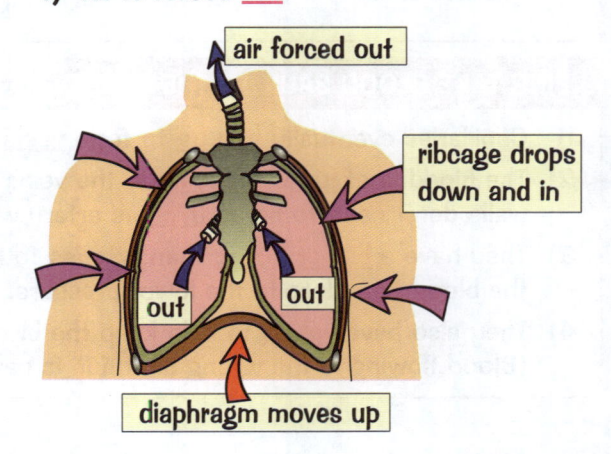

Now take a deep breath and learn these facts...

This is more like it, a bit of proper biology to sink your teeth into — it only gets better from here on in.

Unit 1: Topic 1 — Sport and Fitness

The Blood and Blood Vessels

Now it's time to take a look at blood and just how it's transported round the body...

Blood is a Fluid Made up of Cells, Platelets and Plasma

1) Red blood cells — they transport oxygen from the lungs to all the cells in the body.
2) White blood cells — they help to fight infection.
3) Platelets — these help the blood to clot at the site of a wound.
4) Plasma — this is the liquid that carries everything about, e.g. glucose, carbon dioxide and lactic acid (see the next page).

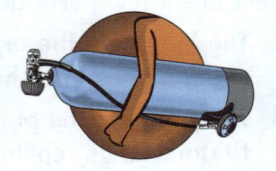

Blood is Carried Around the Body in Blood Vessels

There are three different types of blood vessel:

1) ARTERIES — carry the blood away from the heart.
2) CAPILLARIES — involved in the exchange of materials at the tissues.
3) VEINS — carry the blood to the heart.

Blood Vessels are Designed for Their Function

ARTERIES CARRY BLOOD UNDER PRESSURE

1) The heart pumps the blood out at high pressure, so the artery walls are strong and elastic.
2) The walls are thick compared to the size of the lumen (the hole down the middle). They contain thick layers of muscle to make them strong.

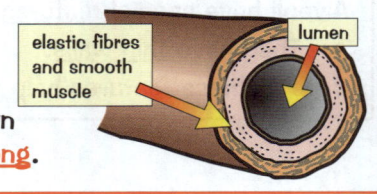

CAPILLARIES ARE REALLY SMALL

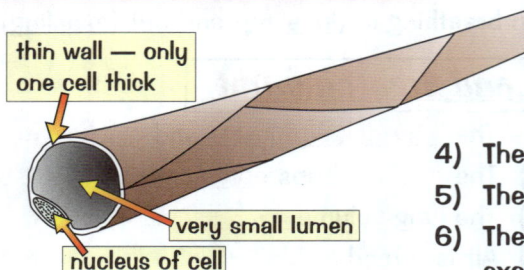

1) Arteries eventually branch into capillaries.
2) Capillaries are really tiny — too small to see.
3) They carry the blood really close to every cell in the body to exchange substances with them.
4) They have permeable walls, so substances can move in and out.
5) They supply food and oxygen and take away wastes like CO_2.
6) Their walls are only one cell thick. This increases the rate of exchange by decreasing the distance over which it happens.

VEINS TAKE BLOOD BACK TO THE HEART

1) Capillaries eventually join up to form veins.
2) The blood is at lower pressure in the veins so the walls don't need to be as thick as artery walls.
3) They have a bigger lumen than arteries to help the blood flow despite the lower pressure.
4) They also have valves to help keep the blood flowing in the right direction. (Blood flowing in the wrong direction is called backflow.)

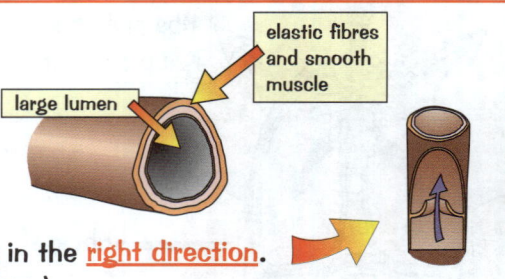

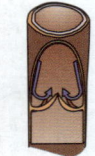

Learn this page — don't struggle in vein...

When you're ill or pregnant the doctor often takes a blood sample for analysis (see p.23). Blood tests are really useful — they can diagnose lots of things because the blood transports lots of chemicals produced by the body.

Unit 1: Topic 1 — Sport and Fitness

The Heart and Respiration

Blood doesn't just move around the body on its own, of course. It needs a pump — that's the heart. Blood is pumped around the body to bring oxygen and glucose to all your cells so they can respire.

Learn This Diagram of the Heart with All Its Labels

1) The right atrium of the heart receives deoxygenated blood (blood without any oxygen) from the body.
2) The deoxygenated blood moves through to the right ventricle, which pumps it to the lungs.
3) The left atrium receives oxygenated blood (oxygen rich blood) from the lungs.
4) The oxygenated blood then moves through to the left ventricle, which pumps it out round the whole body.
5) The left ventricle has a much thicker wall than the right ventricle. It needs more muscle because it has to pump blood around the whole body, whereas the right ventricle only has to pump it to the lungs.
6) The valves prevent the backflow of blood.

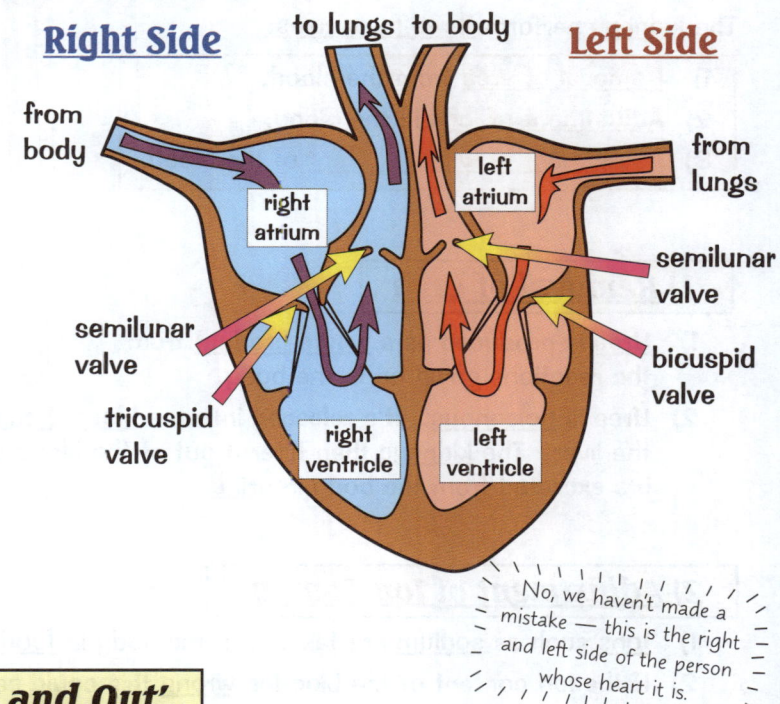

No, we haven't made a mistake — this is the right and left side of the person whose heart it is.

Respiration is NOT 'Breathing In and Out'

Respiration is really important — it releases the energy that cells need to do just about everything.

1) Respiration is the process of breaking down glucose to release energy.
2) It goes on in every cell in your body. When you exercise, a lot of the energy released in respiration is used to make your muscles contract.
3) There are two types of respiration — aerobic and anaerobic.

AEROBIC RESPIRATION NEEDS PLENTY OF OXYGEN

1) Aerobic respiration is what happens when there's plenty of oxygen available.
2) "Aerobic" just means "with oxygen" and it's the most efficient way to release energy from glucose.
3) This is the type of respiration that you're using most of the time. It turns glucose from your food and oxygen from your lungs into carbon dioxide and water — releasing loads of energy in the process:

$$\text{Glucose + Oxygen} \longrightarrow \text{Carbon Dioxide + Water} \quad (+ \text{Energy})$$

ANAEROBIC RESPIRATION DOESN'T USE OXYGEN AT ALL

1) Anaerobic respiration happens when there's not enough oxygen available.
2) "Anaerobic" just means "without oxygen". It's **NOT** the best way to convert glucose into energy because it releases much less energy than aerobic respiration.
3) In anaerobic respiration, the glucose is only partially broken down, and lactic acid is produced.

$$\text{Glucose} \longrightarrow \text{Lactic Acid} \quad (+ \text{Energy})$$

Anaerobic respiration means you can use your muscles for longer during hard exercise.

The waste products of respiration (carbon dioxide and lactic acid) are carried away from your cells in the blood.

Okay — let's get to the heart of the matter...

The human heart beats 100 000 times a day on average. You can measure it by taking your pulse, p.3.

Unit 1: Topic 1 — Sport and Fitness

The Kidneys

The kidneys are really important — they control the content of the blood. Your kidneys can fail though — people with kidney failure can use a kidney dialysis machine to replace some functions of the kidney.

Kidneys Basically Act as Filters to "Clean the Blood"

The kidneys perform three main roles:

1) Removal of urea from the blood.
2) Adjustment of ions in the blood.
3) Adjustment of water content of the blood.

1) Removal of Urea

1) Urea is produced as a waste product from the reactions going on in the body.
2) Urea is poisonous. It's released into the bloodstream by the liver. The kidneys then filter it out of the blood and it's excreted from the body in urine.

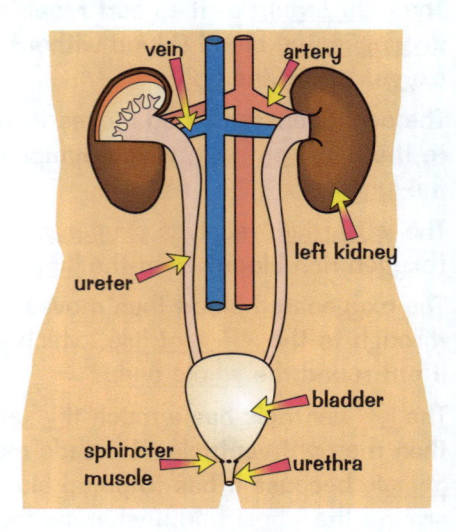

2) Adjustment of Ion Content

1) Ions such as sodium are taken into the body in food and then absorbed into the blood.
2) If the ion content of the blood is wrong this could cause too much water to enter or leave body cells. Having the wrong amount of water can damage cells.
3) Excess ions are removed by the kidneys. For example, a salty meal will contain far too much sodium and so the kidneys will remove the excess sodium ions from the blood.
4) Some ions are also lost in sweat (which tastes salty, you may have noticed).

3) Adjustment of Water Content

Water is taken into the body as food and drink and is lost from the body in three main ways:
1) In urine
2) In sweat
3) In the air we breathe out.

The body has to constantly balance the water coming in against the water going out. Your body can't control how much you lose in your breath, but it can control the other factors. This means the water balance is between:

1) Liquids consumed
2) Amount sweated out
3) Amount excreted by the kidneys in the urine.

On a cold day, if you don't sweat, you'll produce more urine which will be pale and dilute.
On a hot day, you sweat a lot and produce less urine which will be dark-coloured and concentrated.
The water lost when it's hot has to be replaced with water from food and drink to restore the balance.

Adjusting water content — blood, sweat and, erm, wee...

If your kidneys fail, urea, ions and water all accumulate in the blood (this makes sense if you think about it — they're not being filtered out properly). Urea is a poisonous waste product, so having too much of it poisons your body and may even lead to death. Having too much water and too many ions can also cause health problems.

Unit 1: Topic 1 — Sport and Fitness

Joints

Fitness professionals need to understand how we move, so they need to know all about joints...

Joints Allow the Bones to Move

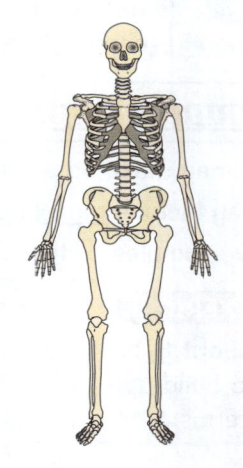

1) The skeleton is a rigid frame for the rest of the body — it supports the soft tissues.
2) It is made up of different kinds of bones that are very tough. They protect delicate organs — like the brain, heart and lungs.
3) Bones move at joints — places where two or more bones meet.
4) Bones on their own can't move though. Muscles, attached by tendons, can move various bones (see below).

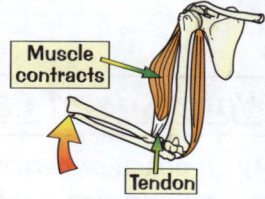

The muscle contracts, pulling on the tendon, which lifts the lower arm.

TENDONS AND MUSCLES
1) Bones are attached to muscles by tendons (which also attach muscles to other muscles).
2) Muscles move bones at a joint by contracting (becoming shorter) and then relaxing (becoming longer).
3) Tendons can't stretch much so when a muscle contracts it pulls on the bone.

LIGAMENTS
1) The bones at a joint are held together by ligaments.
2) Ligaments have tensile strength (i.e. you can pull them and they don't snap easily) but they are pretty elastic (stretchy).
3) They stop the bones in the joint from being dislocated (pulled out of place) when they move.

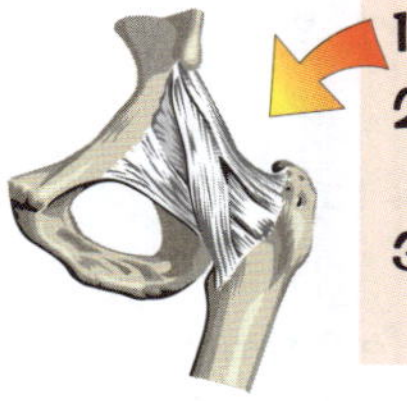

CARTILAGE
Cartilage is a type of tissue that forms a cushion between bones to stop them rubbing.

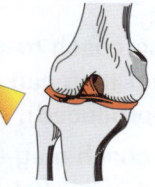

You Need to Know the General Structure of a Joint

Below is a diagram of a knee joint. You need to be able to label the bones, muscles, cartilage, ligaments and tendons on a diagram like this.

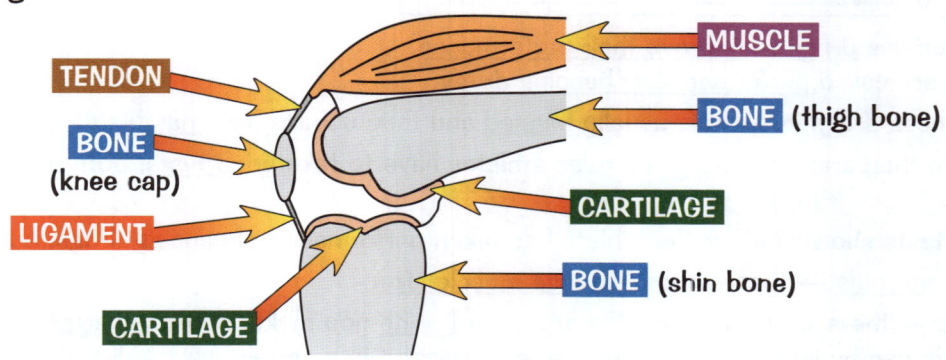

- MUSCLE
- TENDON
- BONE (knee cap)
- BONE (thigh bone)
- LIGAMENT
- CARTILAGE
- CARTILAGE
- BONE (shin bone)

What's a skeleton's favourite instrument?... a trom-bone...

Our bones all meet at joints. Joints are really important because they're where bones can move — otherwise we'd just be playing 'stuck in the mud' all the time. You need to make sure you can label the general structure of a joint and that you know the roles of all the main parts. Then, once you've done that, you can 'move' on...

Unit 1: Topic 1 — Sport and Fitness

Monitoring and Improving Performance

Coaches and personal trainers make up fitness programmes to improve a person's fitness and performance. They need to monitor clients on their fitness programmes for a variety of reasons, e.g. to check they're making progress, to modify (change) the plan if necessary and to provide encouragement.

Fitness Programmes Improve General Fitness

1) A personal trainer may make up a fitness programme to improve a person's general fitness (see p.1).
2) To do this they may include muscle-building exercises and aerobic exercises in the programme.
3) You need to know examples of these exercises, such as:

MUSCLE-BUILDING EXERCISE
Lifting a weight for about 8-12 repetitions (times) to build up the muscles in your arms.

AEROBIC EXERCISE
Running for 20 minutes with your heart rate increased to between 60-80% of its maximum.

Your Speed Can be Monitored

1) A coach or personal trainer can monitor the speed at which a person performs an event (activity), e.g. running a set distance or bowling a cricket ball.
2) To work out the speed they need to know the distance and time of the event.
   E.g. how far a person ran and the time it took them to run that far.
3) Then they use this equation to work out the speed.
   E.g. Anna runs 100 metres in 14 seconds.

   Anna's speed = $\frac{100}{14}$ = 7.1 m/s

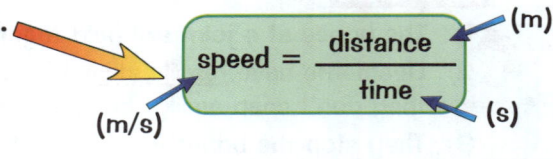

   $$\text{speed (m/s)} = \frac{\text{distance (m)}}{\text{time (s)}}$$

4) The coach may ask the person to repeat the event (e.g. run the same distance again) a few times, so that they can work out an average speed. An average speed is more reliable (it's more likely to be reproduced). E.g. if Anna's speed is repeatedly measured at around 7.1 m/s then it's more reliable.
5) A coach may use a person's event speed to work out what type of sportsperson they should be.
   E.g. a cricket bowler's speed may determine what type of bowler they should train to be.
6) The coach may also monitor a person's event speed over time to see if they are improving, e.g. if a sprinter is getting faster. If they aren't improving, the coach may change their fitness programme.

Taking Drugs Shows up in Urine Tests

1) Some athletes use drugs to improve their performance.
   These drugs are called performance-enhancing drugs.
2) The use of these drugs in sport is usually banned and they usually have nasty side effects.
3) To make sure they aren't breaking the rules athletes have to take urine tests, both during and outside of a competition.
4) These urine tests show whether the athlete has taken performance-enhancing drugs, such as:
   - Anabolic steroids — these drugs increase muscle size.
   - Diuretics — these drugs increase the amount of urine you make, causing weight loss. This can be important if an athlete is competing in a certain weight division.

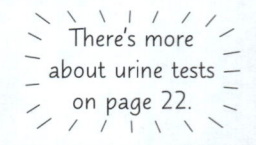

There's more about urine tests on page 22.

Anna Bolic — don't mess with her...

Athletes have to give blood and urine samples to be tested for drugs, like anabolic steroids and diuretics. Testing can happen at any time, and refusing to give a sample can be just as bad as failing a drug test. Punishments for failing a drug test can include lifetime bans from the sport. These drugs can also cause health problems.

Unit 1: Topic 1 — Sport and Fitness

Physiotherapists

There are other jobs in the fitness industry, not just coaches and personal trainers, e.g. like physiotherapists...

Physiotherapists Deal With Skeletal-muscular Injuries by...

...Assessing Them...

1) During sport or when involved in a fitness programme a person may become injured, e.g. they might sprain their ankle.
2) Serious injuries to the skeletal or muscular system can be treated by a physiotherapist.
3) First of all the physiotherapist needs to assess the injury — this means finding out what is injured, the type of injury that has occurred and how bad it is.
4) They'll do this by asking you questions about what you were doing when you injured yourself and what symptoms you have. For example, if you've damaged some cartilage (see p.9) in your knee your symptoms might include pain, swelling and not being able to straighten your leg.
5) A physiotherapist might also need you to have more tests (e.g. an MRI scan) to find out what the problem is.

...Treating Them...

1) A physiotherapist will try to treat the injury. For example, for a sprained ankle, the treatment might involve the RICE method:

> REST — to avoid any further damage. This is especially important for the first 24 hours.
> ICE — to help to reduce swelling (e.g. using a bag of frozen peas wrapped in a tea towel).
> COMPRESSION — a firm bandage is placed around the injured part to help reduce swelling and prevent further damage from excessive movement of the injured joint.
> ELEVATION — raising an injured limb as high as possible to help reduce swelling.

2) Depending on the injury, other possible treatments include cortisone injections to reduce pain and swelling, or laser treatment to speed up healing.

...and Giving Out Sets of Exercises

1) They will also give advice on the best exercises to do to rehabilitate after an injury. These may be graded exercises, which steadily build up the strength of a muscle or joint.
2) For a damaged knee the exercises to strengthen the knee might include:

> 1) Standing up and tensing the muscles without moving the knee.
> 2) Sitting with the lower leg hanging loose, then slowly raising and lowering the lower leg by bending the knee.
> 3) Stepping up and down, onto and off a low box.
> 4) Standing, and bending and straightening the legs at the knees.

If the RICE treatment doesn't work, try noodles...

You can get lots of different types of rice — brown, white, long, short, sticky, egg fried, boiled, steamed, in a bag or as a pudding. But all of this is completely irrelevant, because what you need to know is how physiotherapists assess and treat injuries — oh, and also a set of exercises they might use to treat an injury.

Unit 1: Topic 1 — Sport and Fitness

Fitness Practitioners — Good Practice

A fitness practitioner is a person with special training in fitness. There are many different types of fitness practitioner, e.g. a coach, a personal trainer, a physiotherapist (see previous page). But regardless of their job it's helpful if all fitness practitioners have certain personal qualities and professional skills.

Fitness Practitioners Must be Professional

To be professional they have to follow good practice. This involves...

...developing personal relationships

Fitness practitioners should be able to build up a personal relationship with the patient but remain professional and not become emotionally involved — this could prevent them from making the best decisions.

Trust me, I'm a coach...

...having a good understanding of their area of knowledge

This allows them to make good judgements — they need to be able to tell when the evidence doesn't agree with what the client is saying, e.g. a client might say that they've been sticking to their diet but the scales say they've gained weight, so the evidence doesn't agree.

...considering the whole person

They should be able to consider the whole person — this means taking into account the effects of family, workplace and environment on their clients' health and fitness.

...working as a team

Fitness practitioners have to work well as part of a team. This is because different practitioners will work with a client, e.g. coaches and physiotherapists will have to work together when treating someone recovering from a broken leg.

Following Good Practice Requires Good Communication Skills

Fitness practitioners need good communication skills for a number of reasons:

1) It's important that fitness practitioners are able to explain things in a way that the client understands fully what they have to do or what's going to happen.

2) They also need to be able to ask questions in a way that gets the required information from the client.

3) Communication with other fitness practitioners is important when working as part of a team.

4) Listening skills are important too. Professionals need to be able to understand what the client is saying. Sometimes clients are confused and children can't always explain things — someone else may need to reinterpret what is said.

I'm good at listening (just ignore the snoring)...

These skills are really important for anyone who wants to be a fitness practitioner, but they're also really important for loads of other jobs too, e.g. if you want to join the police or be a chef. Also, if you know why these skills are important it'll help you remember what the skills are. Now onto the next page for a sneaky test...

Unit 1: Topic 1 — Sport and Fitness

Revision Summary

That wasn't such a bad section to start on. Now you know how the human body works and all about the people, organisations and techniques used to keep it fit and healthy, you could almost be a personal trainer yourself. Well, you could if you enjoy doing exercise, rather than cheering other people on from the sidelines or from the other side of the telly (like me). I'm sure being a fan keeps me fit too, all that jumping up and down... Anyway, here are a few questions to check that you do know it.

1) Name a type of fitness facility and describe the services it provides.
2) Name and describe the role of two professionals who work in fitness.
3) Give one example of how health and safety regulations may affect a personal trainer's day-to-day job.
4) Define the following words:
   a) lifestyle,
   b) health,
   c) fitness.
5) Is the number of cigarettes a person smokes per day an example of their lifestyle, health or fitness?
6) Give four lifestyle factors that can negatively affect a person's fitness.
7) Give three basic tests that are part of a baseline assessment.
8) What type of thermometer is a plastic strip that is placed on the skin and changes colour to show temperature?
9) What is a sphygmomanometer used to measure?
10) Describe a test that can be used to measure aerobic fitness.
11)* Cecil is 180 cm tall and weighs 85 kg. Calculate his **BMI**. (Use the equation below.)

$$BMI = \frac{body\ mass}{(height)^2}$$

12) If a person's body mass index is 21 would they be classed as underweight, a healthy weight, overweight or obese?
13) What is the name of the part of the breathing system where gas exchange occurs?
14) Name the four main things the blood is made up of.
15) Describe how the structures of arteries, veins and capillaries are adapted to their function.
16) Name two valves found in the heart.
17) What do the valves in the heart do?
18) Write down the word equation for aerobic respiration.
19) Anaerobic respiration produces energy. What other substance does anaerobic respiration produce?
20) State the three main roles of the kidney.
21) Describe what the following parts of a joint do:
    a) tendons,
    b) muscles,
    c) ligaments.
22) Name the type of tissue that is found between bones to stop them rubbing.
23) Give one example of a muscle-building exercise.
24) Write down the equation for speed.
25)* In a game of tennis Paul serves the ball. The ball travels 11 m in 0.25 seconds. Work out the speed the tennis ball was travelling at.
26) How would a physiotherapist treat a sprained ankle?
27) Name two qualities or skills that fitness practitioners should possess.

* Answers on p.108.

Unit 1: Topic 1 — Sport and Fitness

Organisations Involved in Health Care

Health care is very important for, well, keeping everyone healthy. There are loads of different organisations and services to help with all sorts of health problems. And you lucky ones need to know all about them...

Local Organisations Provide Health Care For the Community

If you ever have any problems with your health (e.g. you feel ill, have toothache or can't stop winking), you can go to your local health care organisation to get help. Because these health care organisations are local, everyone can get to them easily. Different health care organisations provide different services, for example:

HOSPITALS

For most illnesses like an upset tummy or a funny, itchy rash, your general practitioner (GP) will be able to diagnose and prescribe medicines. But for some illnesses patients have to be referred (see page 19) to the local general hospital. They have doctors who specialise in certain areas of treatment, for example:

1) Routine surgery — e.g. having your tonsils removed.
2) Paediatrics — children's medicine.
3) Ophthalmology — if you've got an eye problem.
4) Gastroenterology — if your bowels are causing the problem.

Some hospitals also have an accident and emergency (or casualty) department — these provide emergency treatment for people who have, e.g. broken bones, head injuries, serious wounds etc.

HEALTH CENTRES

A health centre is where many people go to see their GP. But they're not just a doctor's surgery — they also provide other services which don't always involve seeing a doctor. For example you might visit your health centre to:

1) have a blood test (see page 23) carried out by a nurse,
2) get family planning advice,
3) get antenatal care (care during pregnancy) from a midwife (see page 22).

Hospitals and health centres can be run by the NHS (see below) or by private companies (so the patient has to pay for their own care).

There are plenty of other local health care organisations, e.g. opticians (where you go to get your sight and eyes checked) and dentists (where you go to get your teeth and gums checked).

The National Health Service Provides Free Health Care

In the UK, the National Health Service (NHS) is the organisation that's responsible for running hospitals and other health care services, e.g. pharmacy services, general practitioners, health centres, midwives and health visitors. The NHS has some important features:

1) The NHS provides everyone with free health care (unlike in some other countries where you have to pay for it).
2) It provides specialist care that isn't available locally — local hospitals can't treat every medical condition so there are specialist hospitals that provide care nationally. One example is the London Hospital for Tropical Diseases, which treats all sorts of weird infections.
3) It monitors national trends, for example the spread of infectious diseases.
4) The NHS also plans how resources should be distributed — e.g. where to build new hospitals or clinics, how many new staff are needed in an area, what machinery and equipment needs replacing, etc.

The NHS is paid for by taxes.

Gastroenterology — getting to the bottom of the matter...

Don't worry if big words like ophthalmology and gastroenterology are a bit scary — you don't need to learn them. They're just there to show the range of health care services offered by local hospitals. Phewwww.

People Involved in Health Care

It's great having lots of health care organisations but they're not going to run themselves. There are loads of skilled people who work in these organisations providing treatment and generally looking after our health.

There are Lots of People Trained to Provide Health Care

Doctors, dentists, you name it — anyone who calls themselves a health care practitioner has been specially trained to work in health care. They have learned specific scientific and technical skills to do their job, e.g:

A doctor

Doctors diagnose people and decide on the best course of treatment. Doctors may become general practitioners or they may specialise in a particular area of medicine. The skills they need to do their job include:
1) Having an in-depth knowledge of many different diseases and the way the human body works.
2) Being able to interpret the results of tests (e.g. blood and urine tests, see pages 22-23).
3) Having good communication skills so they can inform (tell) a patient about their condition, their treatment and any risks involved (see page 19).
4) Knowing when to refer the patient to another health care practitioner (see p.19).

A nurse

A nurse's role is to care for patients and help them cope with their condition. They may also test, treat and monitor patients, following instructions from a doctor. Nurses may specialise in a particular area of care. The skills they need to do their job include:
1) Having knowledge of diseases and medical problems.
2) Being able to monitor a patient's vital signs (e.g. temperature, heart rate) using special equipment (e.g. a thermometer, a heart rate monitor).
3) Being able to carry out basic tests, e.g. blood tests (see p.23).
4) Having good communication skills to offer support and give medical advice to a patient.

There are loads of other health care practitioners that you're likely to meet too. For example:
1) Dentists — check for and treat any problems with your teeth and gums (they help them to look nice too).
2) Pharmacists — give out medications (drugs) your doctor prescribes (says you can have).
3) Opticians — check for problems with sight and help you to see more clearly (e.g. by giving you glasses).
4) Nutritionists — advise you on the best foods to eat to stay healthy or to reduce symptoms of a disease.

Health Care Practitioners Have Regulations to Follow

Health care practitioners don't just run round doing whatever they want, oh no. They have to follow rules (e.g. Health and Safety regulations) that are set out by the government and other regulators (e.g. the General Medical Council). These rules make sure they're doing their job properly and safely. For example:

- Pharmacists must never give out-of-date medication as it might harm the patient.
- Any health care practitioner coming into contact with a patient's body fluids (e.g. saliva) must wear throwaway gloves. This is to stop any transfer of germs between the patient and the health care practitioner.
- All health care practitioners must keep patient records (the information gathered about a patient) confidential (private) by law.

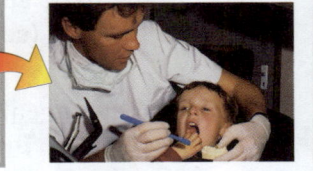

Doctor, Doctor — I swallowed a bone...

Not really, I'm only choking. Anyway, as you can see, there are loads of people that can help you out should you ever have anything wrong with your health. And with all those rules around, you know you'll be in safe hands. Make sure you know the roles of two health care practitioners and the skills they need to do their job.

Unit 1: Topic 2 — Health Care

Public Health

With all the knowledge health care practitioners have, it only seems fair that they share the information around. And they do — through good old talking and public health campaigns they tell us what we need to know.

It's Good for Practitioners to Meet Their Patients Regularly

There are a number of advantages to regular contact between a health care practitioner and their patients.

1) The practitioner can keep up-to-date with the patient's medical history (information on their past and present health problems and treatments). This means the practitioner can give the most appropriate treatment and advice for that patient.

2) Regular appointments allow the practitioner looking after a patient to make sure that a treatment is going well and that the patient is getting better.

3) It also means that the health practitioner and the patient get to know and trust each other. This is important because it makes the patient more relaxed.

Health Education and Information are Important

1) People have a duty to look after their own health as far as possible.

2) Health care organisations and health care practitioners also have a duty to educate and inform the public about matters that affect their health. This helps people to make the right choices for themselves.

3) Information about health is passed to the public in different ways, e.g. through leaflets, TV campaigns and by talking to patients directly.

4) Some information is given to help stop people getting diseases. This also saves the NHS spending money on treatments, so it can be spent on other resources. For example, the public are informed about:

> Lifestyle improvements — people are given advice on how to improve their lifestyle and why (e.g. to stop smoking because smoking causes lung cancer). If people follow the advice they'll be less likely to suffer from diseases and they could live longer.

> Vaccinations — people are told which vaccinations are available and why they should have them. For example, the Department of Health runs campaigns to tell the elderly that they can have the influenza (flu) vaccine, to stop them getting flu. Vaccinations stop diseases spreading, which means fewer people will need treating or die from them.

Percy decided maybe smoking wasn't that cool after all.

5) Information is also given to patients who need medical treatment, so they can make their own decisions about what will be best for them. For example, patients are given information about:

> Available treatments — someone needing treatment should have information on the different types they could have. E.g. a cancer patient could be treated with radiotherapy, chemotherapy or surgery, so they should be told about them all. This means the patient can choose the right treatment for themselves.

> Operation success rates — these rates tell the patient how likely it is a specific type of operation will be a success. The patient needs to be able to weigh up the risks of an operation against its benefits (see p.19) to decide whether to have it or not.

> Post-treatment survival time — some treatments can't cure a person, but may make them live longer. The post-treatment survival time is the amount of time a person is likely to live for after treatment. Patients need to know this to decide whether to have the treatment or not.

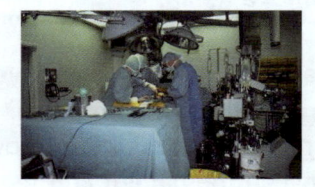

Leaflets — always useful for making paper planes with...

When you're out and about keep your eyes peeled for health promotion campaigns. They're a really important way for health care organisations to get information and advice about health and disease to the public.

Unit 1: Topic 2 — Health Care

Medical History

If you change doctors or get admitted to hospital you'll more than likely be asked loads of questions. Doctors might even go over these questions again when you go in feeling under the weather or before starting a course of treatment. All of the information they collect makes up your medical history.

A Medical History is Information on Your General Health...

Here are some of the questions you'll be asked:

1) "Do you have any symptoms?"

Symptoms are things that a patient feels, such as pain or tiredness. Knowing the symptoms that a patient is suffering from will help a doctor to diagnose any condition they might have.

2) "Are you taking any medication?"

This includes over-the-counter medicines like cold-relief powders as well as prescription drugs. Doctors need to know what medication you're already taking before they can prescribe any other drugs. This is because when some drugs are taken together they can cause nasty side-effects.

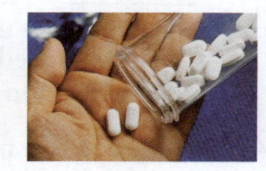

3) "Is there any history of illness in the family?"

If there's a history of certain diseases in your family, this might mean you have a greater chance of developing that disease. Diabetes and heart disease are conditions that 'run in families'.

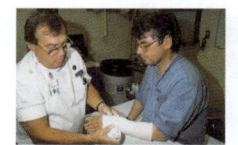

4) "Have you had any previous illnesses or injuries?"

Some symptoms could be related to a previous illness or injury. So knowing what the previous illness or injury was could help with the diagnosis.

5) "Are you allergic to anything?"

An allergy is when the body's immune system reacts to something that isn't really harmful. The body's reaction (called an allergic reaction) can cause dangerous symptoms, e.g. breathing problems. Doctors need to know about a patient's allergies to avoid treatments that could cause an allergic reaction.

...And Your Lifestyle

Here are some more questions you'll be asked:

6) "How much tobacco do you smoke?"

They'll usually want to know if you smoke and, if you do, how many cigarettes you smoke a day. Any symptoms you're suffering could be related to smoking.

7) "How much alcohol do you drink?"

They'll usually want to know how much you drink in a typical week because any symptoms you're suffering from could be related to alcohol intake.

8) "How much exercise do you do?"

This might be how many hours you spend in the gym or it might be how far you walk or cycle in a typical day. Exercise has an impact on general health and fitness.

Me? — I run at least 10 miles a day...

Remember, the person who takes your medical history isn't spying on you — they need to know this information to plan the best treatment for you. It doesn't help anyone if you tell fibs so you seem healthier than you are.

Unit 1: Topic 2 — Health Care

Prioritising Treatment and Resources

When lots of people need treatment, medical staff must be able to respond quickly and make sure the right people are seen to first. They also need to have the right type and right amount of resources to do this.

In Emergency Care it's Important Who's Treated First

1) When emergency care is needed it's important for health care professionals to prioritise treatment — this is done using a process called triage.
2) Triage means assessing patients' injuries, and deciding who needs help first and who can wait a little longer to be helped.
3) The location of the emergency affects who is responsible for prioritising care:

'A and E' means accident and emergency.

At the scene of an accident (e.g. a bus crash):
Paramedics are trained medical staff who travel to emergencies in ambulances. They are usually the first people who need to prioritise treatment, including which patients need to be taken to hospital and in which order.

In an A and E department:
When people arrive at emergency departments, specialist nurses called triage nurses decide who should be treated first.

4) Paramedics and triage nurses assess a patient by checking their vital signs (e.g. temperature, pulse rate, breathing rate, blood pressure, whether the person is conscious or not). If the patient's vital signs are out of the normal range (e.g. their pulse is too weak, their breaths are too shallow), this could mean they're seriously injured and so they need to be treated first.
5) Patients with major blood loss, head injuries or serious broken bones are treated next.
6) People with minor injuries, like cuts or bruises, are treated last.
7) Elderly patients and young children are also given priority over people with the same severity of injury, as they're generally weaker.
8) Time is really important — the quicker someone is treated the better their chances of survival.

A and E Departments Have to Manage Their Resources

A and E departments need lots of resources (e.g. staff, equipment, medicines), which cost money. The department only has a limited amount of money, so they have to manage their resources very carefully. This is so patients are given the best care possible in the most efficient way (i.e. without wasting any resources). There are several ways they do this:

1) Triage systems — by prioritising patients (see above), resources go where they need to first and are less likely to be wasted.
2) Practice for major incidents — staff have training sessions where they practice for emergencies, like a road traffic accident. The staff learn what they have to do, how to use equipment and where everything is etc. This means when there's a real emergency, the department will be well-prepared so resources won't be wasted.
3) Staff — there needs to be enough staff in the A and E department to treat the predicted number of patients it will get each day, but not too many. Too many staff means money is wasted. Instead it's better to have more staff at home on stand-by who can be called on if they're needed.
4) Equipment — there's got to be enough equipment to deal with the number of patients needing help. Equipment is expensive though, so departments must make sure they don't waste money getting more than they need. E.g. there's no point in an A and E department having 50 beds if there's only ever been 15 patients in the department at once.

Ey Andy, can you help me please?

In an emergency there's none of this first come first served business. If you turn up at A and E with a splinter in your thumb on the same day that a train's come off its tracks, you might be in for a bit of a wait. Although you could think back to this wonderful page while you're waiting to understand why you're just not a priority.

Unit 1: Topic 2 — Health Care

Treatment

Doctors and other health care practitioners will advise you on the most appropriate form of treatment for your problem. But the treatment will only go ahead if you're happy with the plan and if you give your consent.

GPs Can Refer You to Other Health Care Practitioners

If you have a problem with your general health (e.g. a sore throat, tummy ache or an itchy bum) your GP would be the best person to go to first. If they can't make a diagnosis or can't confirm it, they might refer you to a specialist service for further tests.

A fertility clinic is a clinic that can help a woman get pregnant.

> For example, if a couple were struggling to get pregnant they might go to their GP. The GP might then refer the couple to a fertility clinic for further tests to find out why.

Once a GP has diagnosed your problem they might still need to refer you to a specialist service for treatment.

> For example, a GP might diagnose a woman as being infertile (meaning she can't get pregnant naturally). If the woman and her partner want children, the GP may then refer them to a fertility clinic where she could have IVF treatment (see page 21).

Diagnostic Procedures and Treatments Can Be Risky

1) Diagnostic procedures are the tests a patient has to help a doctor diagnose their problem, e.g. X-rays, blood tests. They are done to help the patient but they can also carry some risk.

> For example, x-rays use radiation, so having an x-ray could slightly increase your risk of getting cancer.

2) Treatments are designed to cure or reduce the symptoms of a disease or health problem, e.g. an injury. All forms of treatment have associated risks.

> For example, there are lots of risks associated with surgery — complications on the operating table, the risk of picking up a serious bacterial infection, or the patient reacting badly to the anaesthetic.

3) The patient has to weigh up the benefits and risks against each other. If they feel the benefits outweigh the risks they are likely to go ahead with the diagnostic procedure or treatment.

> For example, x-rays can show up serious injuries (e.g. broken bones), which means the benefit usually outweighs the risk (a slightly increased chance of getting cancer).

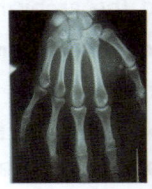

Patients Have to Give Their Consent

1) Because of the risks involved with diagnostic procedures and treatments (see above), informed consent (permission to do it) must be given by a patient before they begin.
2) The health care practitioner has to tell the patient all about the procedure or the treatment, the risks involved, the benefits and any alternatives.
3) If the patient decides to go ahead they may have to sign a consent form.

Revision can be risky — you might overheat your brain cells...

If your GP sends you off to see other people, don't take it personally — they're just trying to get you the most suitable sort of help for your problem. And remember, when it comes to tests and treatments there are always both benefits and risks to be weighed up. Aaah — it's hard work being a patient these days, so many decisions.

Unit 1: Topic 2 — Health Care

Pregnancy

Pregnancy involves the growth of a new life inside a female body. It's not surprising that it brings about lots of changes in a woman's body (and I'm not just talking about a sticky-out belly button and stretch marks)...

The Female Reproductive System Makes Eggs (ova)

1) An egg (ovum) is produced every 28 days from one of the two ovaries.
2) It passes into the oviduct (fallopian tube) where it may meet sperm, which have entered the vagina during sexual intercourse.
3) Fertilisation happens when the nucleus in the egg and the nucleus in a sperm cell fuse (join) together.
4) If it isn't fertilised by sperm, the egg will break up and pass out of the vagina.
5) If it is fertilised the new cell will travel down the fallopian tube to the uterus (womb). It will then attach itself to the endometrium (uterus lining) — this is called implantation. The new cell then begins to grow and develop into a fetus (baby).

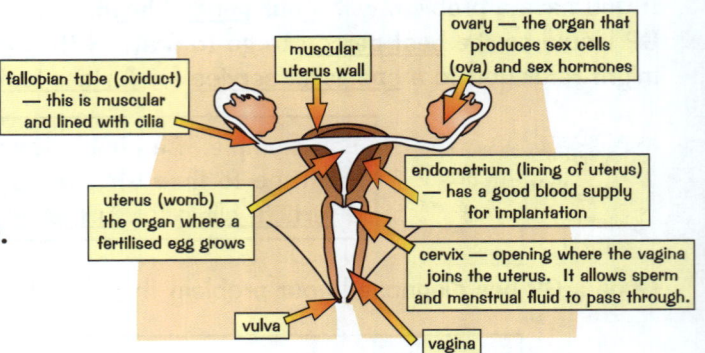

Diagram labels:
- muscular uterus wall
- fallopian tube (oviduct) — this is muscular and lined with cilia
- ovary — the organ that produces sex cells (ova) and sex hormones
- endometrium (lining of uterus) — has a good blood supply for implantation
- uterus (womb) — the organ where a fertilised egg grows
- cervix — opening where the vagina joins the uterus. It allows sperm and menstrual fluid to pass through.
- vulva
- vagina

The Female Body Changes During Pregnancy and Birth

Changes during pregnancy

1) Uterus stretches — to allow room for the fetus (baby) to grow.
2) Amnion membrane forms — this surrounds the fetus and is full of amniotic fluid to protect the fetus against knocks and bumps.
3) Placenta develops — this lets the blood of the fetus and mother get very close to allow the exchange of food, oxygen and waste.
4) Umbilical cord develops — to connect the placenta to the fetus.
5) Breasts enlarge — the breasts get ready to start producing milk.

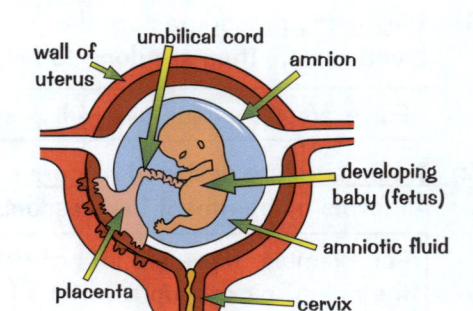

Diagram labels: wall of uterus, umbilical cord, amnion, developing baby (fetus), amniotic fluid, placenta, cervix

Changes during birth

1) Amnion breaks — and the amniotic fluid flows out.
2) Cervix dilates — the cervix widens ready for the baby to come out.
3) Uterus contracts — the muscles of the uterus start to contract to push the baby out.
4) Placenta comes out — after the baby is born the placenta comes away from the lining of the uterus and is pushed out of the body (called the afterbirth).
5) Milk is produced — to provide the new baby with food.

This is what women are talking about when they say 'my waters have broken'.

The Female Body Functions Differently During Pregnancy

Carrying a baby can be hard work for the body:
1) The mum puts on weight — due to a larger uterus and breasts, and extra fat stored for breast feeding.
2) Heart rate increases — to help supply the body with all the extra energy it needs.
3) The kidneys have to work harder — to filter the extra waste that's coming from the baby.

Female or not — you've still got to know all this...

Pregnancy is tough going — it's nine months of flippin' hard work for a woman's body. You need to know all the bits and bobs that make up the female reproductive system, and how it changes during pregnancy and birth.

Unit 1: Topic 2 — Health Care

IVF

Sometimes couples who can't get pregnant seek medical treatment to help nature along a bit.

IVF Can Help Couples to Have Children

IVF means "*in vitro* fertilisation". It's a way of fertilising an egg in a laboratory. Couples who can't get pregnant naturally (through sexual intercourse) may be referred by their GP to a fertility clinic to get IVF (see page 19). Here's what happens during IVF:

1) **Hormone treatment** — IVF starts with giving the woman hormones to stimulate her egg production. This means she has lots of eggs available for the clinic to try to fertilise.

2) **Egg collection** — next eggs are collected from the woman's ovaries. This involves having a needle inserted into the top of her vagina which 'sucks' the eggs out.

3) **Fertilisation** — the collected eggs are then fertilised in a lab using the man's sperm. These are then grown into embryos.

4) Once the embryos are tiny balls of cells, one or two of them are transferred to the woman's uterus.

5) **Implantation** — after a few days the embryos may implant into the lining of the uterus where they can grow into a baby as in a normal pregnancy. The woman may be given more hormones at this stage to reduce the chance of miscarriage (losing the baby).

Some couples can get IVF free on the NHS but other couples have to pay for it privately.

IVF Increases the Chance of Having Twins (or Triplets, or More...)

1) When an embryo is transferred into the woman's body it doesn't always implant and make her pregnant.
2) During IVF more than one embryo is transferred at a time to increase the chance of pregnancy.
3) If all the embryos implant and start growing, the woman will have multiple babies (e.g. twins).
4) A woman will find out how many babies she is carrying when she is monitored during her pregnancy (e.g. during an ultrasound scan — see page 22).

Couples Who Have IVF Often Have Counselling

IVF can put a big strain on a couple. They may need counselling to help them cope with the treatment, and the emotions and problems it brings, e.g:

Counselling is talking to a person who is trained to give support and advice about many issues.

1) **Worries** — couples can have counselling before treatment starts so they know what to expect. This helps them to prepare for the treatment and the emotions that they're likely to go through.
2) **Stress** — waiting to find out whether IVF has worked can take over a couple's life. Also IVF is very expensive (unless the couple can get it on the NHS), so money worries can add to the stress. Counselling can teach a couple methods to cope with stress.
3) **Guilt** — one member of the couple may feel it's their fault that they can't have a baby together. Counselling can help the person deal with this.

What's an IVF surgeon's favourite drink — fertili-tea...

In a nutshell, the main stages of IVF are hormone treatment, egg collection, fertilisation and implantation, which make a baby (or two) — make sure you know them all. Couples also have counselling to help them through it.

Unit 1: Topic 2 — Health Care

Antenatal Care

It's far from easy growing a whole new person. No wonder so many people help to look after you when you're pregnant. GPs, midwives and doctors all get to have a good poke around to check everything's going well.

Women Get Antenatal Care While They're Pregnant

Antenatal care is the care a woman gets when she's pregnant. It involves lots of tests and appointments to check on her health and the health of her growing baby. Women generally get their antenatal care from a midwife (although GPs sometimes provide part of the antenatal care too). The role of a midwife providing antenatal care includes:

1) Taking a medical history (see page 17) from the mother so they can find out if there's anything that might make the pregnancy risky (e.g. a previous miscarriage).
2) Informing the mother about the antenatal care she'll be offered so she knows what to expect.
3) Doing routine tests to check on the health of the mother and baby (see below).
4) Informing the mother about the risks of pregnancy (see below) and symptoms she should look out for.

There Are Loads of Checks to be Done at Antenatal Appointments

URINE SAMPLES
The mother is usually asked to bring a urine sample to every antenatal appointment. The results of a urine test can show up health problems — see below.

MOTHER'S WEIGHT
A woman will usually only be weighed at the start of her pregnancy. Being overweight or underweight can increase the risk of problems (during pregnancy and the birth) for both the mother and baby.

BLOOD PRESSURE
Blood pressure will be monitored at every antenatal appointment. High blood pressure can be very dangerous for the mother and baby (see below).

ULTRASOUNDS
Women generally have two ultrasound scans during their pregnancy. During an ultrasound scan sound waves are sent through the woman's abdomen (belly). These get turned into images on a monitor (so you can see the baby). Ultrasound scans are used to check the baby is growing normally and to work out when it's due.

Women May Develop Diabetes During Pregnancy...

1) Diabetes is a condition in which the body can't control its blood sugar (glucose) level properly.
2) Sometimes this develops for the first time during pregnancy — this is known as gestational diabetes.
3) A high level of glucose in a urine sample can show that a woman has gestational diabetes.
4) Blood tests can confirm that she has the condition (if there are high levels of glucose in the blood).
5) Gestational diabetes increases the risk that the baby will be born with health problems. It can also increase the size of the baby, which can cause problems for mother and baby during the birth.

...Or Dangerously High Blood Pressure

1) Pre-eclampsia is an illness that a mother can develop during pregnancy.
2) Women with pre-eclampsia develop high blood pressure and have protein in their urine — so it's usually detected when blood pressure and urine samples are checked.
3) Pre-eclampsia can lead to very serious problems for the mother, e.g. liver, kidney and lung problems.
4) It can also lead to health problems for the baby as it gets less oxygen and nutrients while it's growing.

I don't have an Aunty Natal, but I do have an Aunty Sue...

A pregnant woman may become sick of the sight of her midwife because she has so many checks. But these checks mean that problems like gestational diabetes and pre-eclampsia can be picked up early and treated.

Unit 1: Topic 2 — Health Care

Blood Tests

People have blood tests for all kinds of reasons. For example, a pregnant woman may have blood tests as part of her antenatal care (see page 22) to check that both her and the baby are healthy.

To Have a Blood Test You Need to Give a Sample of Your Blood

There are lots of people qualified to take samples of your blood (e.g. doctors, nurses and midwives). If you've never had a blood sample taken before, this is what you can expect:

1) Firstly, a tight band (tourniquet) will be put around your upper arm. This makes the veins in your arm (below the band) fill with blood, so they'll bulge and be easier to see. Lovely.
2) The person taking your blood will then look for a nice, juicy vein close to the surface of the skin to take blood from. This will usually be on the inside of your elbow.
3) They'll then wipe an area of your vein with an antiseptic wipe to sterilise it.
4) Next they'll do the blood sucking bit. A sterile needle (attached to a sterile syringe) will be inserted into your vein. As they pull up the plunger, the syringe will fill with blood.

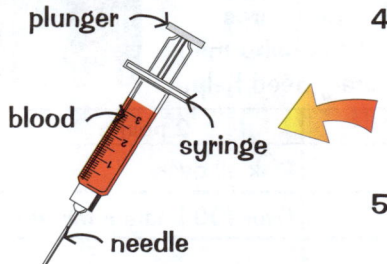

If something's 'sterile' or has been 'sterilised' it means it's free from microorganisms (e.g. bacteria). These could cause disease if they got into your bloodstream.

5) Then the needle will be taken out of your vein and you'll get a sterile plaster to cover the wound (you might get a lollipop at this point or a smiley face sticker — if you're seven that is...).
6) Finally they'll transfer the blood they've taken into a sample tube. This has to be clearly labelled with your details (e.g. name, date of birth) so your blood doesn't get mixed up with somebody else's and you get given the wrong results.

Blood Tests Are Common in Pregnancy to Identify Problems

Blood tests during pregnancy help to diagnose health problems with the mother and can show whether the baby will be born with a birth defect (a physical health problem that is there from birth), such as:

ANAEMIA

1) Anaemia is a lack of iron in the blood.
2) It makes the mother feel tired and worn out.
3) Iron is found in red blood cells (see p.6).
4) Blood tests can give information about a mother's red blood cells, e.g. the number of them, their size and shape. If the results are not normal she may have anaemia.

SPINA BIFIDA

1) Spina bifida is a birth defect that affects the spinal cord (long bundle of nerve fibres that runs down your back next to the spine).
2) Children with spina bifida often have trouble moving around and learning things.
3) A woman's blood can be tested for a protein called alpha fetoprotein (AFP) while she is pregnant. High levels of AFP may mean that her baby will be born with spina bifida.

DOWN'S SYNDROME

1) Down's syndrome is a birth defect that affects the way a child develops.
2) Children with Down's syndrome often have learning problems and they're more at risk of other health problems, e.g. heart disease, hearing problems.
3) An unborn baby with Down's syndrome will pass different amounts of some proteins and hormones to their mother during pregnancy compared to a healthy baby. So to test whether a baby is at risk of being born with Down's syndrome, the mother's blood can be tested for:
   - high levels of hormones hCG (human chorionic gonadotrophin) and inhibin A,
   - low levels of hormone uE3 (unconjugated oestriol) and protein AFP (alpha fetoprotein).

Blood test — all you have to do is sit still, now that's my kinda test...

You're very likely to have a blood test at some point in your life, so it's good to know the six steps involved in giving a blood sample. And it'll help you pick up marks should it crop up in the exam too — always a bonus.

Unit 1: Topic 2 — Health Care

Post-Natal Care

Once a baby's born there are health care practitioners there to check the little bambino's as healthy as can be.

A Baby Gets Post-Natal Care After It's Born

Post-natal care is care after birth. It involves checking and testing the baby to make sure it's healthy. For about the first ten days after birth, post-natal care is given by a midwife. After this a health visitor takes over the care. A health visitor is a trained nurse that works in the community. Parents can take babies to see their health visitor at local clinics, e.g. at a health centre (see p.14). There are lots of checks done on a baby:

A Baby's Health is Checked As Soon As It's Born

One minute and five minutes after the baby's born, it's given a score to rate its health. The score is worked out (usually by a midwife) using the APGAR scale. The APGAR scale measures Appearance, Pulse, Grimace, Activity and Respiration. The scores are added together. A score over 8 is good. A score of 5-7 is fair but the baby may need some help breathing. A score under 4 means the baby will definitely need help.

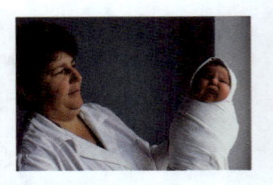

Point score	0 points	1 point	2 points
Appearance	Blue all over	Blue hands and feet	Pink all over
Pulse	No pulse	Under 100 beats a minute	Over 100 beats a minute
Grimace (reflex response)	No response to stimulation	Whimpers slightly in response or pulls a face	Cries loudly and coughs
Activity	Limp and floppy muscles	Some movement of arms and legs	Moving well
Respiration	Not breathing	Weak or irregular	Breathing well and crying

Health Visitors Carry Out Development Tests

1) Babies have their physical development tested at about 10 days old and 6-8 weeks old.
2) This means that any problems with development can be picked up as early as possible.

Health visitors check a baby's...
- Weight and length.
- Responses to light and sound.
- Motor skills (how well they can move their body).

A Baby's Growth is Monitored

1) A baby's growth is regularly monitored after birth to make sure it's growing normally and provide an early warning of any growth problems. Three measurements are taken — length, mass (weight) and head size. These results are plotted on average growth charts like this...
For example, the blue cross on this growth chart shows a 6 month old baby that weighs 6 kg.
2) The chart shows a number of 'percentiles'. E.g. the 50th percentile shows the mass that 50% of babies will have reached at a certain age.
3) Babies vary in size, so doctors aren't usually concerned unless a baby's size is above the 98th percentile or below the 2nd percentile (red lines on the graph), or if there's an inconsistent pattern (e.g. a very small baby with a very large head). For example, the baby shown by the blue cross on the chart wouldn't concern doctors because its size is on the 25th percentile. But the baby shown by the purple cross might set alarm bells ringing because it's above the 98th percentile.

I was born to be a footballer — I scored 7 as soon as I was born...

Once the baby's out there are just a few more checks to make sure everything's okay. The end of the baby checks and the end of the section. Hoorah. On to some summary questions to check you know your stuff.

Unit 1: Topic 2 — Health Care

Revision Summary

That was quite an interesting section really. Now you know about all about the organisations and people that keep you healthy. And you know what your mum went through to bring you into this world. Heck, you could almost be a health care practitioner (well, maybe after your A-levels and then years at Uni, but let's not dwell on details). Here are a few questions to check that you do know it...

1) Name two types of local health care organisations and describe the services each one provides.
2) Describe three features of the National Health Service.
3) For two different health care practitioners:
   a) describe their role,
   b) describe two skills they need to do their job.
4) Give one example of a rule a health care practitioner needs to follow to help them carry out their job safely.
5) Give two reasons why it's good for practitioners to meet their patients regularly.
6) Give two things the public is informed about to help stop people from getting diseases.
7) Explain why a patient needing medical treatment may be told about post-treatment survival time.
8) List three questions a health care practitioner might ask you when taking a medical history.
9) What does triage mean?
10)*The following people are brought into the accident and emergency department of a hospital after being involved in a car accident.
    Susan (26) has a few cuts and bruises but no major injuries.
    Gareth (27) is complaining of chest pains and has difficulty breathing.
    Gerald (74) is complaining of chest pains and has difficulty breathing.
    Angela (31) has lost quite a bit of blood but the bleeding has been stopped.
    In what order should the casualties be treated?
11) Briefly describe two ways that an accident and emergency department might manage its resources.
12) Give two reasons why a GP might refer a patient to a specialist service.
13) Why might a patient start a treatment even though it carries a risk to their health?
14) What information should a patient get about a diagnostic procedure before they give informed consent?
15) What does a fertilised egg travel down to get to the uterus?
16) Describe two changes that happen to the body during pregnancy.
17) Describe what happens to the amnion during birth.
18) Describe the process of IVF.
19) Why is it more likely that IVF will result in multiple births compared to a natural pregnancy?
20) Give two reasons why couples having IVF might need counselling.
21) Describe two things a midwife does.
22) Give four checks that might be done at an antenatal appointment.
23) Give two ways in which gestational diabetes is detected.
24) What substance is a mother's urine tested for to help diagnose pre-eclampsia?
25) Explain why pre-eclampsia can be bad for a baby.
26) Why is a tight band used when a blood sample's being taken from your arm?
27) When a blood sample's being taken, describe what happens after the blood has been drawn into the syringe.
28) List two birth defects that blood tests during pregnancy can help to detect.
29) Describe what is meant by 'post-natal care'.
30) What does APGAR stand for?
31) List three things that are checked during a baby's post-natal development tests.
32) Why is a baby's growth regularly monitored?

* Answers on p.108.

Unit 1: Topic 3 — Protecting the Environment

Scientists and Environmental Protection

You need to know about the people and organisations that help keep an eye out for our environment. Luckily I've written this excellent page covering just that. What a coincidence.

There are Organisations that Look After the Environment

The Environment Agency is a government-funded organisation that aims to make the environment a better place for people and wildlife — for example by:

1) Monitoring industrial sites — e.g. checking that factories aren't causing too much pollution and that waste is being disposed of (got rid of) properly.
2) Collecting data on water pollution and monitoring flood risks.
3) Monitoring air quality.
4) Protecting wildlife.

Environmental Protection Officers Protect the Environment...

1) Environmental protection officers are scientists who work for organisations like the Environment Agency. They collect and analyse evidence about the environment, and do work that protects and improves our environment.

2) Environmental protection officers work outdoors, in laboratories and in offices. They need different scientific and technical skills, including:

- A thorough understanding of environmental science and laws relating to the environment.
- Good data collection skills, including knowing how to collect, store and prepare samples (evidence) for analysis (see page 28).
- A knowledge of good laboratory practice to help them produce reliable results in the lab (see page 27).
- Keen observational skills to help them gather and examine visual evidence (see page 29).
- Good communication skills to enable them to communicate their findings to others.

...and Are Affected By Regulations

1) Environmental protection officers must follow Health and Safety regulations to keep themselves and others safe while they work. These regulations vary depending on whether they're working in a laboratory or outside. E.g. in a laboratory, an environmental protection officer might need to wear a lab coat to protect their clothes. On an industrial site, they might need to wear a hard hat to protect their head.

2) Environmental protection officers also make sure regulations to do with the environment are stuck to, e.g. laws about pollution and waste disposal. The Environment Agency takes legal action against offenders who break environmental protection laws.

Clean your room — protect the environment...

Environmental protection officers (and organisations like the Environment Agency) do a great job at helping to keep our rivers clean, our wildlife happy and our air fresher than a daisy. Without them we'd probably be knee-deep in nappies, old car tyres and industrial waste. So three cheers for them I say. Hip hip...

Good Laboratory Practice

Good laboratory practice is needed to produce and analyse reliable results.

Results Need to be Reliable

Reliable results come from experiments that give the same data:

- each time the experiment is repeated,
- each time the experiment is reproduced (copied) by other scientists.

Good Laboratory Practice Increases Reliability

Good laboratory practice makes it more likely that results will be both repeatable and reproducible. This makes them more reliable. It involves:

1) Using common practices and procedures — this means that different scientists and different laboratories perform experiments, like testing water quality, in the same way.
2) Following health and safety regulations — like wearing protective clothing and disposing of chemical waste properly. This reduces the chance of samples being contaminated, which can invalidate results.
3) Checking and maintaining all equipment regularly — so the equipment is kept in good condition and is able to produce reliable measurements and results.
4) Training staff and offering continued professional development — so staff always know about the latest and best methods to use.

Proficiency Tests are Used to Check Reliability

Proficiency testing compares test results from different labs to check they're reliable. Proficiency testing can be used to:

1) Check that a lab can do standard tests.
2) Check the performance of individual workers.
3) Check that instruments are working properly.
4) Look at new test methods.

In proficiency testing, different laboratories are sent samples of the same material to test. The reliability is checked by comparing results from the different laboratories — each lab is sent a sample of the same material so they should all get the same results.

Public Labs are Accredited to Show Their Results are Accurate

1) Public laboratories can be accredited — in the UK by UKAS (United Kingdom Accreditation Service).
2) Accreditation shows that the lab meets internationally agreed standards, the staff should always work to a good level and the results produced should be accurate (close to the true answer) and precise (close to the average).
3) This means anyone looking at the results from an accredited lab can be pretty sure that the experiments were carried out in a standard way, so they can have confidence in the results.

Tamoto techkup — a sauce of error...

There are loads of great reasons to learn good laboratory practice — passing your GCSE exams for one.

Unit 1: Topic 3 — Protecting the Environment

Taking Samples

Environmental scientists often need to collect samples of things like soil and water for analysis back in the lab. Anyone collecting samples must follow the same stages of collection, storage and preparation.

Samples Need to be Carefully Collected, Stored and Prepared

Here are the main stages involved:

1) **Collecting representative samples.** The more samples you take, the more representative they'll be of whatever it is you're sampling — this will make your results more reliable.

> For example, if you want to know how polluted a stretch of river is, it's no good taking a sample from just the one spot — the level of pollution there might be much higher or lower than it is anywhere else. It's better to take lots of samples at random points along the river and compare the results from each one — this will give you a better idea about what the whole stretch of river is like.

2) **Avoiding contamination.** You need to make sure that your samples don't become contaminated, e.g. with bacteria, chemicals or other samples. This means collecting your samples using sterile equipment and then sealing them in separate, sterile containers.

3) **Labelling samples.** You need to label your samples to avoid confusion back at the lab. The label should say exactly what the sample is of, as well as where and when it was taken.

4) **Storing samples.** You need to store your samples properly to prevent them changing or deteriorating (losing quality) before they can be analysed. How you store the samples will depend on what they are. Keeping samples in a fridge can help to slow down chemical reactions and the growth of bacteria.

5) **Keeping samples safe.** You don't want anyone tampering (messing) with the samples as this could change the results of the analysis. Samples might need to be kept locked away and signed in and out of storage.

Sampling Living Organisms Can Help to Monitor Climate Change

The temperature of the Earth is gradually increasing. This is a type of climate change and it's having a serious effect on the oceans. Scientists can assess this effect by monitoring ocean organisms. For example:

1) High temperatures make ice caps melt. This is causing some animals to lose their habitat, e.g. the Pacific walrus. Scientists may monitor the number and distribution of these animals to see how climate change is affecting them.

2) Sea temperatures are rising. This can cause coral bleaching — where corals lose their colour and may die. This is bad news for the fish and other organisms that feed off them. Scientists record the amount of coral bleaching to assess the impact climate change is having on coral reefs.

Indicator Organisms Can Be Used to Show Water Pollution

An indicator organism is an organism that shows whether an area is polluted or not, e.g. an area of freshwater.

1) Some organisms can only survive in unpolluted conditions, so if you find lots of them, you know it's a clean area.

> Mayfly and stonefly larvae can't survive in polluted water. The cleaner the water, the more larvae survive.

Freshwater areas include ponds, streams, rivers and canals.

2) Other organisms have adapted to live in polluted conditions — so if you see a lot of them you know there's a problem.

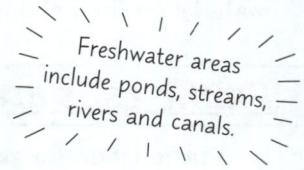

> Water lice, rat-tailed maggots and sludge worms all indicate polluted water. But out of these, rat-tailed maggots and sludge worms indicate a very high level of pollution.

Indicator organisms — animals to help you turn left...

Rat-tailed maggots, nice... still, that's no excuse for not learning this page — this stuff could easily be in your exam.

Unit 1: Topic 3 — Protecting the Environment

Visual Examination

Visual examination is a simple, quick and low-tech method of examining evidence. It's often used by environmental protection officers when they're out and about, e.g. when they're investigating a flood site.

A Permanent Record is Made During a Visual Examination

When a scientist visually examines evidence, a permanent record must be taken for future use.
This can be done by:
1) Writing a description.
2) Drawing pictures.
3) Taking photographs.
4) Recording a video.

For example, an environmental protection officer investigating a site that's been flooded might make a drawing of the area before taking photos or recording a video of the damage that's been done. They might then write a report describing what they've found.

There Are Some Important Features to Look Out For in Visual Images...

1) **Sharpness of focus** — how blurry an image is.

2) **Magnification** — the relationship between the size of an object in the image and its actual size. A high magnification makes an object look bigger than it actually is.

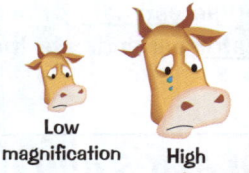

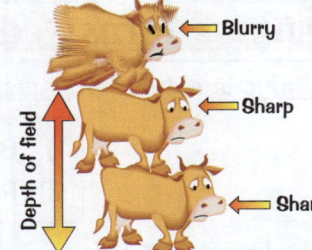

3) **Depth of field** — the distance between objects in the image that are in focus.

4) **Contrast** — the difference between the colours in an image. The higher the contrast, the more objects stand out.

These features affect how you interpret the evidence from an image. E.g. if the magnification isn't high enough, you might not be able to see enough detail. If the contrast is too low, key objects might not stand out.

Objects and Images Can be Compared to See If They Match

1) Visual examinations are often used to compare pieces of evidence to see if they match. The important features are compared to see what points are the same or different, e.g. the pattern of a footprint found at a crime scene may be compared to the pattern of a footprint made by some suspects' shoes.

2) Often the best way to compare things is to record the size by measuring it with a ruler or tape measure, e.g. using a measuring tape that has 1 cm graduations, if the top of a footprint is half-way between the 25th and 26th graduation, it's approximately 25.5 cm long.

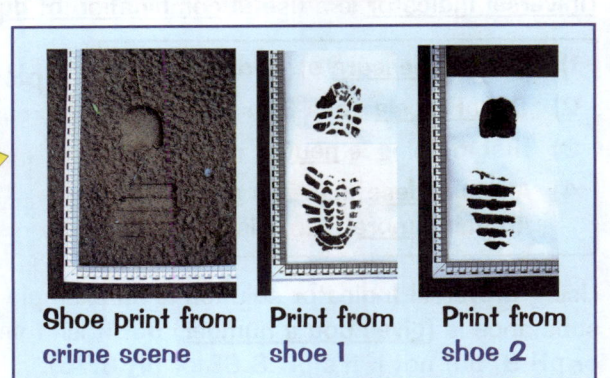

3) In some cases the area needs to be calculated. E.g. the area of an oil slick may be measured to tell how bad the spill is. Areas are calculated using formulas:
- The area of a square or rectangle = length × width
- The area of a circle = $\pi \times r^2$ (where r = radius)

Measurements May Vary

1) It's important to remember that if you take a lot of measurements of the same thing (e.g. the area of an oil slick), you won't always get the same result. This could be because the conditions you're taking your measurements in change, or you've made a mistake when measuring (human error).

2) Because measurements of the same thing always vary to some extent, an individual measurement might not be the true value of the quantity you're measuring.

Unit 1: Topic 3 — Protecting the Environment

Types of Testing

Much like examiners, scientists just love to test things. And they've got different ways of doing it.

There are Three Types of Testing Techniques...

Qualitative
These tests usually give you a yes/no answer (they don't give you a number answer).
E.g. litmus paper can tell you whether a substance is an acid or an alkali (see below).

Quantitative
These tests measure something and give you an accurate number.
E.g. pH can be measured accurately using a pH meter (to within 0.1 pH units).

Semi-Quantitative
These tests give you an estimate of something (but they aren't as accurate as quantitative tests).
E.g. Universal Indicator can indicate the pH of a solution to within 1 or 2 pH units (see below).

Litmus Turns Red in Acids and Blue in Alkalis

Litmus is a dye that changes colour in acids and alkalis. It's put onto filter paper so it can be used easily.

1) Blue litmus paper turns red in acids.
2) Red litmus paper turns blue in alkalis.

Acid   Alkali

The litmus test tells you whether a sample is an acid or an alkali.
It doesn't tell you how much acid or alkali is present — so it's an example of a qualitative test.

Universal Indicator Estimates pH

Universal Indicator is a useful combination of dyes that's used to estimate the pH of a substance.

1) pH is a measure of acidity.
2) The pH scale goes from 0 to 14.
3) If something is neutral it is pH 7.
4) Anything less than 7 is acidic.
   Anything more than 7 is alkaline.

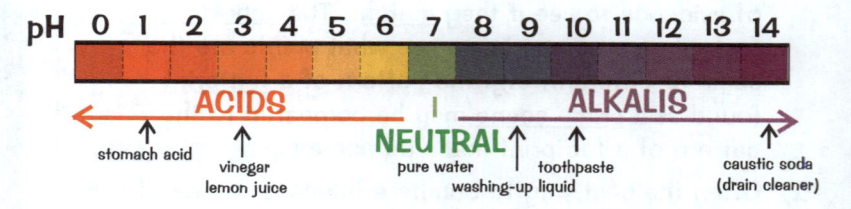

pH 0 1 2 3 4 5 6 7 8 9 10 11 12 13 14

← ACIDS | ALKALIS →
stomach acid, vinegar, lemon juice — NEUTRAL, pure water — toothpaste, washing-up liquid, caustic soda (drain cleaner)

Using Universal Indicator solution is an example of a semi-quantitative test — it tells you how acidic a substance is (gives you a number) but it isn't very precise (e.g. it can only tell you if something is pH 8 or pH 9, but not if it's pH 8.65 or pH 8.75).

Test Kits Can be Used to Monitor the Environment

Environmental protection officers often use test kits to help them investigate things like water quality (see next page) and the level of minerals in soils. E.g. a semi-quantitative test kit for a particular soil mineral would tell you whether the mineral was present in small, medium or large quantities.

Exams — your very own testing technique...

Remember: qualitative tests tell you about something's qualities. Quantitative tests tell you about quantities (amounts). And semi-quantitative tests are a sort of a wishy-washy in between. Don't get them mixed up.

Unit 1: Topic 3 — Protecting the Environment

Testing Water Quality

Environmental protection officers often need to assess water quality. Yawn. One way of doing this is to look at what's floating around in it. And I'm not talking about ducks.

Solids Can be Dissolved or Suspended in Water

If you take a sample of water from a river or stream, it won't be pure water. Instead, it'll have solids dissolved or suspended in it.

Dissolved solids

1) Some solids dissolve when you mix them with water — you can tell they've dissolved when you can't see them any more.
2) The water and dissolved solids form a solution.
3) Solutions can be clear (see-through).
4) Many salts dissolve in water to form a clear solution.
5) If you filter a solution, you won't be able to separate the solids from the water.

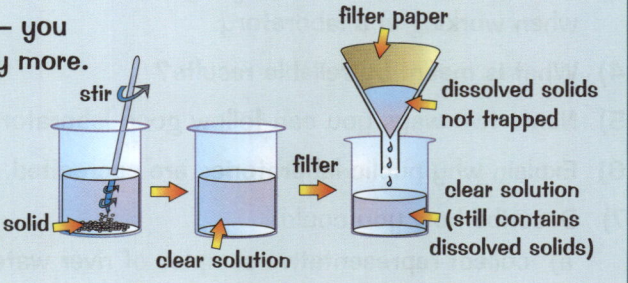

Suspended solids

1) Suspended solids mix with water, but they don't dissolve in it — you can still see them floating about.
2) The small solid particles make the water look cloudy.
3) Suspended solids include things like mud, sand and clay.
4) They can be separated from water using filter paper.

Turbidity is a Measure of the Cloudiness of a Liquid

1) Turbidity is just how cloudy a liquid is — the more suspended solids in a liquid the more cloudy it will be.
2) Turbidity can be measured using a turbidity meter. This measures the amount of light that travels through a liquid. The more cloudy a liquid is, the less light can pass through it.
3) Another way to measure the turbidity of water is to use a turbidity tube:
   - A turbidity tube is a clear tube with a black mark at the bottom.
   - To use it, you need to be looking down into the tube from above. As you do so, you slowly pour a sample of water into the tube until the black mark disappears.
   - You then record the level of water in the tube and use it to calculate the turbidity of the water.

Measuring turbidity is a way of assessing water quality. Water with lots of suspended solids in it isn't great for drinking, and it isn't great for the wildlife living in it. E.g. if the amount of light travelling through the water is too low, plants won't be able to photosynthesise. This will reduce the amount of oxygen in the water for other organisms.

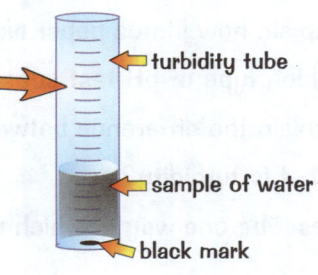

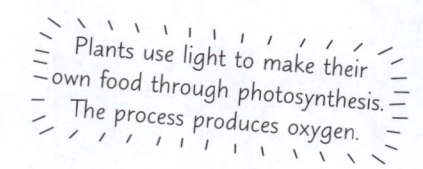

Plants use light to make their own food through photosynthesis. The process produces oxygen.

Don't let this page cloud your judgement...

Make sure you get the difference between dissolved solids and suspended solids straight in your head. You can't see dissolved solids in solution. You can see suspended solids — they make water look cloudy. Turbidity is a measure of that cloudiness. There. What could be simpler. Now onto the revision summary...

Unit 1: Topic 3 — Protecting the Environment

Revision Summary

My favourite part of any section — the end. But it's not over yet for all you budding environmental protection officers. Before you start cracking open the orange squash and having a flick through the TV guide, there's still this revision summary to get through. If your memory fails you, then have a look back through the section. You need to know every last detail.

1) Name one organisation an environmental protection officer may work for.
2) Give two skills needed by environmental protection officers to do their job.
3) Name one health and safety regulation that an environmental protection officer may have to follow when working in a laboratory.
4) What is meant by reliable results?
5) Name two ways you can follow good laboratory practice.
6) Explain why public laboratories are accredited.
7) Describe how you could:
    a) collect representative samples of river water,
    b) avoid contamination of your samples,
    c) prevent someone from tampering with your samples.
8) Give one example of how sampling living organisms can help scientists to monitor climate change.
9) Explain how you could use indicator organisms to tell whether an area of freshwater was polluted.
10) Give two ways you could make a permanent record during a visual examination.
11) What is:
    a) the magnification of an image?
    b) the contrast of an image?
12) Write down the formula for calculating:
    a) the area of a square,
    b) the area of a circle.
13) Explain why measurements of the same thing will always vary to some extent.
14) Explain the difference between qualitative, quantitative and semi-quantitative tests.
15) Explain how litmus paper works.
16) Which type of pH test substance, litmus or Universal Indicator, gives a purely qualitative result?
17) Explain the difference between solids that are dissolved in water and solids that are suspended in water.
18) What is turbidity?
19) Describe one way in which you could measure turbidity.

Unit 1: Topic 3 — *Protecting the Environment*

Unit 1: Topic 4 — Protecting the Public

Scientists Protecting the Public

You might not realise it, but scientists play an important role in keeping us safe and sound...

Public Analysts Work in Consumer Protection...

1) Public analysts make sure that things used by the public meet certain safety standards and laws. This includes food, drinking water, toys, cosmetics and medicines.
2) They work in local authorities and in organisations like the Food Standards Agency. They often work alongside laboratory technicians.
3) The roles of a public analyst include:

   - Monitoring food safety and making sure health and safety standards are met.
   - Providing advice on and research into food-borne diseases (caused by eating contaminated food).
   - Making sure products are labelled correctly.
   - Ensuring food safety legislation (see below) is kept to.

4) Public analysts often play an important role in local communities, e.g. by inspecting local factories or collecting and analysing samples from local food outlets.

...and Need a Scientific Background

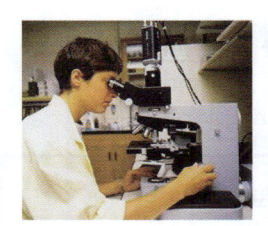

Public analysts need the following skills to do their job:
1) They need a good understanding of analytical techniques such as colorimetry (see p.34) and chromatography (see p.35). They may also need to be able to interpret images from microscopes (see p.37).
2) Public analysts working in the food industry also need to be familiar with the latest food safety legislation — these are laws regulating the safety, quality and labelling of food on sale to the public.

SOCOs and Forensic Scientists Work in Law Enforcement

1) Scene of crime officers (SOCOs) work closely with the police to record the details of a crime scene and collect any useful evidence.
2) Forensic scientists analyse and examine evidence that might be useful for solving crimes — they work in laboratories and appear as witnesses in court.
3) Many forensic scientists used to work for the Forensic Science Service — a government-owned company that supplied forensic science services to police forces in England and Wales.
4) The Forensic Science Service was closed in March 2012. The services it provided are now carried out by private companies, such as LGC Forensics.
5) The forensic science services offered by these companies include things like:

   - Collecting evidence, e.g. fingerprints, hairs and blood samples.
   - Analysing evidence, e.g. comparing fingerprints and running DNA profiles (see pages 38-39).
   - Recording and preserving evidence.

   The collection, storage and preparation of samples is covered on page 28.

6) Like public analysts, scene of crime officers and forensic scientists need a good understanding of analytical techniques. They also need good observational skills to help them to collect and interpret evidence (see pages 29 and 38).

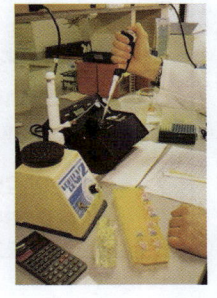

It's just like on TV...

...the forensic science stuff that is. You don't get that many TV programmes about public analysts. Hmmm, I wonder why that is... Anyway, make sure you know this page inside out and top to bottom before you move on.

Colorimetry

Colorimetry is used for measuring colour — which is a lot more useful than it sounds, I promise. It's used to work out how much of a coloured chemical is in a solution. Hold onto your hats folks, here comes the fun...

Colorimeters Measure the Intensity of Colour

Colorimeters are machines that measure colour. They work like this:

1) Light is passed through a solution.
2) Some of the light is absorbed by the solution — darker colours absorb more light than lighter colours.
3) The colorimeter measures the amount of light that passes through the solution and uses this to work out how much light was absorbed.
4) A reading of absorbance is given (the amount of light absorbed).
5) The higher the absorbance, the darker the colour of the solution.
6) Colorimetry can tell you the concentration of a chemical in a solution — it gives you a number, so it's a quantitative test.

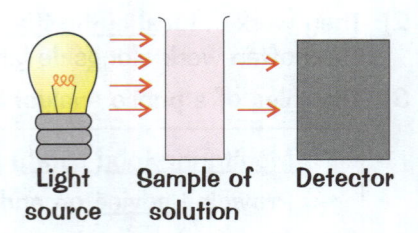

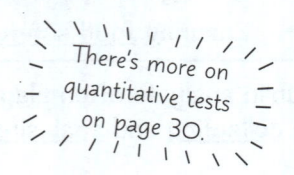

There's more on quantitative tests on page 30.

Samples are Compared to Standard Reference Solutions

You can work out the concentration of a coloured chemical in a solution by comparing it to reference solutions using a colorimeter. Reference solutions are samples of known concentration. To find the unknown concentration of a sample, you have to draw a calibration graph. Here's an example:

An environmental scientist needs to know the concentration of iron in a sample of polluted water.

1) The scientist mixes the water with a chemical that turns red when iron is present. The darker the red colour, the more iron is present.
2) She then puts a colourless solvent (pure water) in the colorimeter to set the meter to zero.
3) She measures the absorbance of some reference solutions and plots the absorbance readings against the known concentrations.
4) Next a line of best fit is drawn — this is a line that goes through, or as near to, as many of the points as possible.
5) Then she tests the polluted water in the colorimeter. It has an absorbance reading of 0.8.
6) She uses the calibration graph to work out the concentration of iron — she draws a line from the absorbance reading across to the line of best fit, then draws a line down and reads off the concentration.
7) The concentration of iron in the polluted water is just under 5 parts per million — 5 parts of iron in a total of 1 million parts.

Did you hear about the biologist that had twins?*

You may have to draw a calibration graph in the exam or use one to work out the concentration of a solution — so make sure you understand how to use them. If you're asked to draw a graph, remember that concentration goes on the bottom (X) axis and absorbance goes up the side (on the Y axis). Then you'll be sorted my friend.

Unit 1: Topic 4 — Protecting the Public   *She called one Henry and the other Reference Sample.

Chromatography

Chromatography is used a lot in the chemical industry — it's a method for separating chemical mixtures. It's pretty useful in forensics, e.g. to compare ink samples to detect forgeries (fake documents).

Chromatography Can be Used to Detect Forgeries

Chromatography is a qualitative test. It can be used to analyse loads of different unknown mixtures, e.g. identifying banned colours in food, a source of pollution in a lake, or the inks used in a suspected forgery. Most inks are made up of a mixture of dyes. A forged document will probably use different ink from an official document (so it'll contain a different mixture of dyes).

Here's how you do paper chromatography...

1) Draw a line across the bottom of a sheet of filter paper (in pencil).
2) Add spots of ink to the line at regular intervals.
3) Tape the top of the paper to a pencil and hang the sheet in a beaker of solvent, e.g. water.

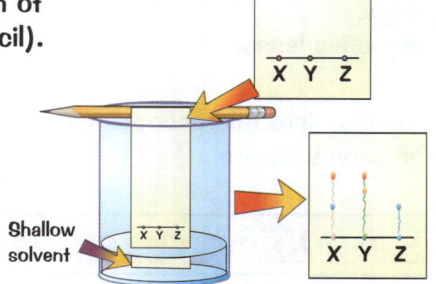

4) The solvent used depends on what's being tested. Some compounds dissolve well in water, but sometimes other (non-aqueous) solvents, like ethanol, need to be used.
5) The solvent seeps up the paper, carrying the ink dyes with it.
6) Each different dye will move up the paper at a different rate and form a spot in a different place.

Thin-Layer Chromatography (TLC) is very similar to paper chromatography. The main difference is that instead of paper it uses a thin layer of gel or paste (e.g. silica gel) on a glass plate.

In both types of chromatography the dyes are separated by the movement of a solvent (called the mobile phase) through a medium of filter paper or gel (called the stationary phase). The dyes move between the mobile and stationary phases as they move up the paper (or gel). The pattern of spots produced by chromatography is called a chromatogram.

Unknown Compounds are Compared to Reference Material

You can compare the dyes in an unknown ink to the dyes in known inks to see which ink it is. The pattern of dye spots will match when two inks are the same (the spots will be the same distance apart).

Some of the spots on the chromatogram might be colourless. If so, you might need to develop the chromatogram — this involves using a chemical called a developer to make the spots coloured (so you can see them).

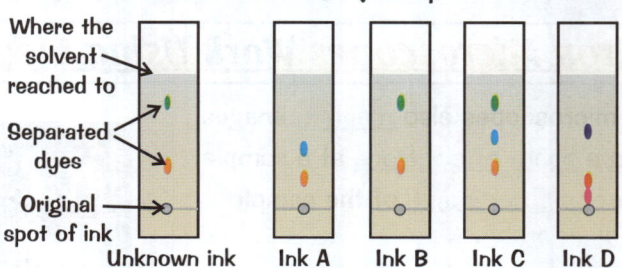

You can see from the position of the spots on the filter paper that the unknown ink has the same composition as ink B.

You can Calculate the R_f Value for Each Chemical

An R_f value is the ratio between the distance travelled by the dissolved substance and the distance travelled by the solvent. You can find them using the formula:

$$R_f = \frac{\text{distance travelled by substance}}{\text{distance travelled by solvent}}$$

So the R_f value for this chemical is B ÷ A.

The R_f value can be matched to a standard value and used to identify the colour in the substance.

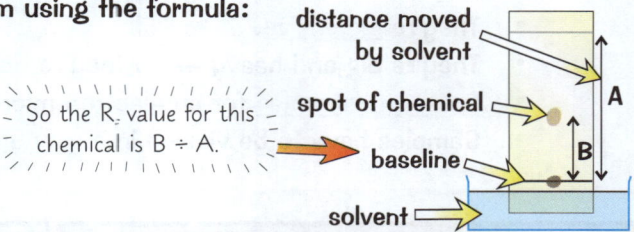

Comb-atography — identifies mysterious things in your hair...

You need to be able to calculate R_f values in the exam — so make sure you learn that formula off by heart.

Unit 1: Topic 4 — Protecting the Public

Microscopes

Microscopes make little things look bigger, so you can see them in more detail. Useful, huh.

Light Microscopes Work Using Lenses

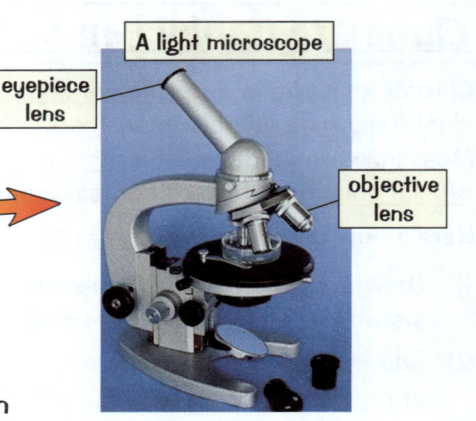

1) Light microscopes use lenses to magnify images. This means they make them look bigger. E.g. if a lens has a '×10' magnification, it makes something look ten times bigger.
2) A light microscope has two types of lens:
   - Eyepiece lens — looked through to see the image and also magnifies the image.
   - Objective lens — magnifies the image. Usually there are three different objective lenses (e.g. ×4, ×10 and ×40).
3) By increasing the magnification of an image, light microscopes can be used to see more detail than can be seen with the naked eye.

A light microscope — eyepiece lens, objective lens

Magnifying Power is Eyepiece × Objective Lens Magnification

You can work out the magnifying power of a light microscope by multiplying the magnification of the eyepiece lens by the magnification of the objective lens:

Magnifying Power = Eyepiece Lens Magnification × Objective Lens Magnification

For example:

Eyepiece lens magnification	Objective lens magnification	Magnifying power
×10	×4	×40
×10	×10	×100
×10	×40	×400

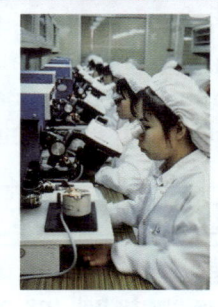

A typical team of scientists at work with their jolly microscopes — remember, there's no 'I' in 'team'.

Scanning Electron Microscopes Work Using Electrons

1) Scanning electron microscopes also magnify images.
2) They work by firing a beam of electrons at a sample.
3) They then create a computer image of the sample called an electron micrograph.
4) Scanning electron microscopes have a much higher magnification than light microscopes. This means that they show loads more detail.
5) They do have a few disadvantages though:
   - They're expensive.
   - They're big and heavy — so they're not very portable.
   - Preparing samples for an electron microscope can be complicated.
   - Samples have to be viewed in a vacuum, i.e. without any air. This kills living samples.

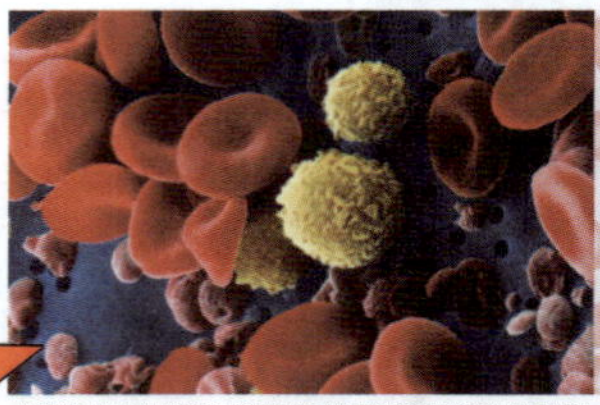

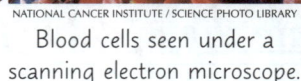

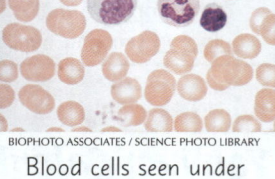

Blood cells seen under a scanning electron microscope.
Blood cells seen under a light microscope.

Elect Ron Microscope — your Science Party candidate...

Scanning electron microscopes produce some pretty cool pictures and they allow scientists to look at tiny objects (like blood cells, see above) in loads of detail. But a good one costs upwards of £150 000. Ouch.

Unit 1: Topic 4 — Protecting the Public

Interpreting Images from Microscopes

Just like a forensic scientist or a public analyst, you need to be able to interpret images from microscopes.

You Might Have to Interpret Images from a Light Microscope...

In the exam you may have to look at a drawing, sketch or photograph from a light microscope, together with a scale, and answer questions about the different features you can see. Here are two examples:

Example 1: This slide shows bacteria found in a sample of food collected by a food hygiene inspector.

1) First describe the main features of the slide.
   - Three different types of bacteria are shown — A, B and C.
2) Then count the numbers of different features.
   - There are — 3 of A, 4 of B and 3 of C.
3) Next measure all the main features.
   - A have a diameter of about 1 μm. B are about 1½ μm long and less than ½ μm wide. C are about 2 μm long and 1 μm wide.
4) Finally identify the features using reference samples.
   - A are cocci. B are bacilli. C are bacilli with flagella.

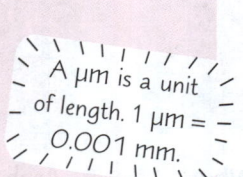

A μm is a unit of length. 1 μm = 0.001 mm.

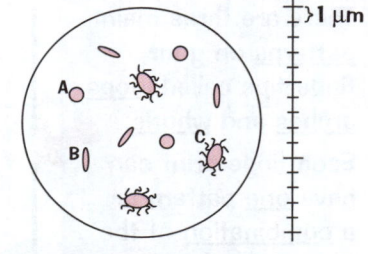

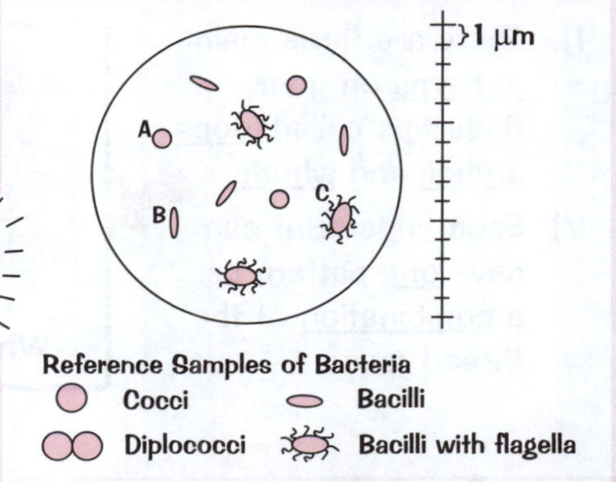

Reference Samples of Bacteria
- Cocci
- Bacilli
- Diplococci
- Bacilli with flagella

Example 2: This picture shows a bullet found by a scene of crime officer.

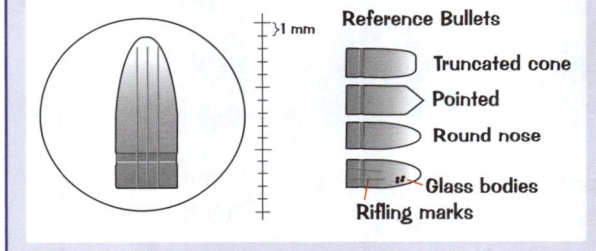

Reference Bullets
- Truncated cone
- Pointed
- Round nose
- Glass bodies
- Rifling marks

1) Describe the main features.
   - rounded tip and lines along its length.
2) Count the numbers of features.
   - three straight lines.
3) Measure the main features.
   - about 12 mm long and 5 mm wide, and the lines are about 1 mm apart.
4) Identify the features using reference samples.
   - round-nosed bullet with rifling marks.

...and from a Scanning Electron Microscope

You interpret a scanning electron micrograph in the same way as a picture from a light microscope. Here's an example I made earlier:

The scanning electron micrograph below shows a sample of pollen from the back garden of a house that was burgled. Pollen are big enough to be seen under a light microscope but to identify the different types of pollen you need to use an electron microscope to get a detailed picture of the surface of the pollen.

1) Describe the main features
   — there are three different types of pollen.
2) Count the number of different features
   — 8 of A, 3 of B and 1 of C.
3) Make measurements of the main features
   — A is 7.5 μm, B is 15 μm, C is 17.5 μm
4) Use reference samples to identify the main features — A is daisy pollen, B is hornbeam tree pollen and C is cherry blossom pollen.

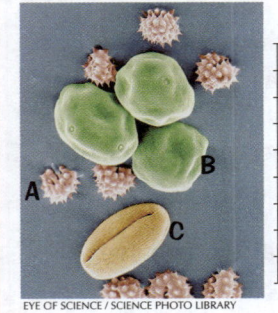

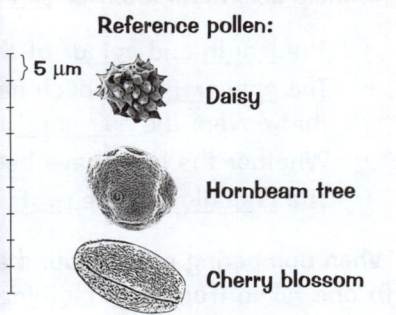

Reference pollen:
- Daisy
- Hornbeam tree
- Cherry blossom

Scanning electron microscopes can't see colour — this picture has had false colour added to make it easier to identify the features.

Revise this — and make light work of it in the exam...

Remember: describe, count, measure and then compare to a reference sample. What on earth could be easier...

Unit 1: Topic 4 — Protecting the Public

More on Visual Examination

Scene of crime officers often use visual examination to help them collect evidence. They examine the crime scene for things like fingerprints, hairs and clothing fibres. It's just like CSI.

Fingerprints Have Three Types of Pattern

The ridges of skin on your fingertips have distinctive patterns. When you touch something you leave a print of the pattern (in sweat... yuk) on the surface you touched. This is called a fingerprint. You need to be able to identify the important features in an image of a fingerprint for the exam:

1) There are three main patterns on your fingertips called loops, arches and whorls.

2) Each fingerprint can have one pattern or a combination of the three types.

Whorl — Arch — Loop

3) The type of pattern and the location of the pattern on the fingertip are different for every person (even identical twins have different fingerprints), which means that fingerprints are unique.

4) Each of your fingers also has a different fingerprint.

A Fingerprint Can Be Compared with Those of the Suspects

1) A fingerprint by itself isn't very useful. It doesn't tell you whose it is — you need to compare it to other fingerprints, e.g. a suspect's fingerprints. This is done by a fingerprint specialist, who looks for matching patterns.

2) No two images of the same fingerprint will look exactly the same, e.g. part of one print may be missing or faint compared to the other print. Because of this fingerprint specialists look for an acceptable match.

Here's an example:

Fingerprint from crime scene — Suspect 1's fingerprint — Suspect 2's fingerprint

The loop on the fingerprint from the crime scene matches the loop on Suspect 2's fingerprint.

Microscopes Are Used to Examine Hairs and Fibres

1) Forensic scientists often analyse hairs and fibres found at a crime scene to see if they could belong to a suspect. To do this, they look at them under a microscope.

2) When comparing a hair found at a crime scene to one taken from a suspect, forensic scientists look for similarities and differences between, e.g.

- The length and colour of the hairs.
- The appearance of each hair's cuticle — a scaly layer that covers the hair shaft.
- Whether the hairs have been dyed or bleached.
- The condition of the roots and tips.

3) When comparing a fibre found at a crime scene to one taken from, e.g. clothing belonging to the suspect, forensic scientists look at things like:

- The width and colour of the fibres.
- How smooth the fibres appear.
- Whether the fibres are twisted or straight.

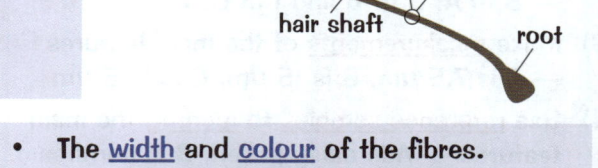

Clothing materials like wool and cotton are made up of fibres.

tip — cuticle — hair shaft — root

Fingerprint specialists have a whorl of a time...

In the exam, you might be asked to compare two images, e.g. of two hairs, to see if they're an acceptable match.

Unit 1: Topic 4 — Protecting the Public

Electrophoresis

Electrophoresis is another really useful technique — it lets you produce a DNA profile. DNA profiles can be used by the police to catch criminals who leave DNA at the scene of a crime, which is handy.

All Organisms Contain DNA

1) DNA is the genetic material found in every cell nucleus. It's like a blueprint for how to make an organism.
2) DNA in humans is unique — no two humans in the world have the same DNA (with the exception of identical twins, who have identical DNA).
3) DNA can be extracted from small biological samples, e.g. hair, blood, and saliva, because they contain cells.

DNA Profiling Can Pinpoint an Individual or Organism

1) DNA taken from a crime scene is usually compared with a DNA sample taken from a suspect. It can be used to link a suspect to the crime scene, or to help prove a suspect wasn't at the crime scene.
2) It can also be used in paternity tests — to check if a man is the father of a particular child.
3) Whatever's being tested the method used is pretty much the same — good old electrophoresis.

HOW IT WORKS

1) First you have to extract the DNA from the cells in the blood, etc.
2) The DNA is then cut up into fragments, producing lots of different sized bits of DNA.
3) The bits of DNA are suspended in a gel, and an electric current is passed through the gel. This separates the fragments.
4) The DNA is then treated to make it visible.

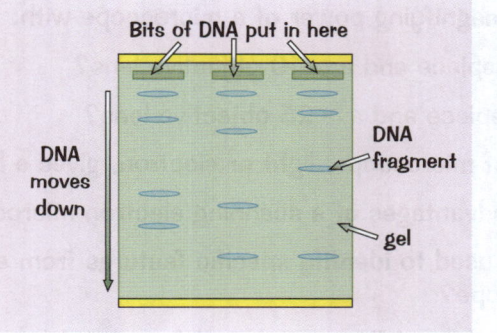

Here's an example:
1) A drop of blood was found at a crime scene.
2) Forensic scientists ran a DNA profile for the blood.
3) They also ran DNA profiles for two suspects.
4) Matching DNA samples have the same pattern of bands. So here you can see that the blood from the crime scene has come from suspect 2.

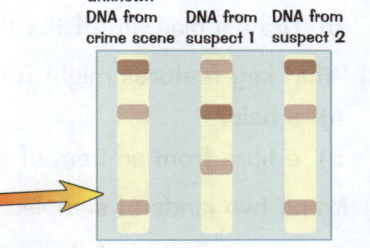

DNA Profiling Technology Has Helped to Improve Law Enforcement

DNA profiling is a relatively modern technology. Before DNA profiling was developed, it was much harder to prove that a particular suspect was or wasn't at a crime scene, so some crimes remain unsolved (even if there was quite a likely suspect). With DNA profiling, some unsolved crimes from years ago can now be solved. This is because DNA can be found on evidence from years or even decades ago and matched to a suspect — as long as the evidence was properly collected and stored in the first place, and hasn't been contaminated.

There Are Ethical Issues Involved with Collecting and Storing DNA

1) Some people would like there to be a national DNA database of everyone in the country.
2) That way, DNA from a crime scene could be checked against everyone in the country to see whose it was.
3) But others think this is a big invasion of privacy. They worry about how safe the data would be and what else it might be used for.

So the trick is — frame your twin and they'll never get you...

DNA profiling hasn't just helped catch lots of criminals — it's helped people to prove their innocence too.

Unit 1: Topic 4 — Protecting the Public

Revision Summary

Phew. There's a lot to get your head around in this section, but you really do need to learn it all for the exam. Use the questions below to check what you do know and what you don't. If there's one you can't answer, go back to the page and have another look. It's the only way I'm afraid...

1) Describe two roles of a public analyst.
2) What skills might a public analyst need to do their job?
3) Describe the role of a scene of crime officer.
4) What does a colorimeter measure?
5) Are the results from a colorimetry test qualitative, semi-quantitative or quantitative?
6) Explain why a reference solution is needed for colorimetry.
7) How are dyes separated in chromatography?
8) Why might some chromatograms need to be developed?
9)* What is the R_f value of a chemical that moves 4.5 cm when the solvent moves 12 cm?
10) What does it mean if a lens has a magnification of ×10?
11)* What is the magnifying power of a microscope with:
    a) a ×10 eyepiece and a ×40 objective lens?
    b) a ×8 eyepiece and a ×25 objective lens?
12) Which type of microscope, light or electron, gives a higher magnification?
13) Give two disadvantages of a scanning electron microscope.
14) What can be used to identify specific features from a picture or photograph from a light microscope?
15) a) Name the three different types of fingerprint pattern.
    b) Draw a diagram of the three different types of fingerprint pattern.
16) What key features might forensic scientists look for in a magnified image of:
    a) a hair?
    b) a fibre from an item of clothing?
17) Name two kinds of samples that DNA can be extracted from.
18) Give one example of the use of DNA profiling in fighting crime.
19) What is the name of the method used in DNA profiling to separate the DNA pieces?
20) Give two ethical issues involved in collecting and storing DNA.

* Answers on page 108.

Unit 1: Topic 4 — Protecting the Public

Unit 2: Topic 1 — Sports Equipment

Designing Sports Equipment

Like any other product, it's important that sports equipment works, that it's safe, and that it won't fall apart straight away. So the people who make it need to think carefully about the materials it's made from...

You Need to Know About Materials Used to Design Sports Equipment

Material scientists and designers of sports equipment need a good knowledge of materials and their properties (see pages 45-46). They also need different scientific and technical skills to carry out their jobs. For example...

1) Material scientists test the properties of different materials in the laboratory (see page 43). They need to know how to carry out these tests safely and how to produce reliable results. They also need to be able to interpret their results (which often involves using a bit of maths).

2) Designers of sports equipment need to be creative and good at problem solving. They have to be able to pick the best material for the product they're making (see pages 45-46). They also need a good knowledge of product standards and safety regulations (see below).

Products Need to be Safe — and Work Properly Too

1) You'd be cross if a product didn't do its job properly, or broke after only a few days.
2) A badly made product might also be dangerous.
3) That's why it's important for designers to make sure their products meet certain basic standards.

Some Organisations Help to Promote Good Standards

There are three main organisations that help to ensure good standards.

1) The British Standards Institution (BSI) produces standards labelled with 'BS' and a number. Each standard is a document describing how well a product should do its job, how safe it should be, etc.

   This is the BSI Kitemark. If a product displays this logo, then it has been tested by the BSI to make sure it conforms to the BSI standards the manufacturer says it does.

2) The European Committee for Standardisation. A product marked 'CE' means that it meets European legal requirements, which include some basic European standards.

3) The International Organisation for Standardisation (ISO) develops international standards, which can be used throughout the world.

Products Must Remain Safe Even in Exceptional Circumstances

Although you can't guarantee that something could never be dangerous, you can build in a safety margin. A safety margin means that a product is designed to be safe even in conditions much more extreme than normal use.

Example: The ropes used by rock climbers are designed to withstand forces greater than normal during a fall.

CGP books — promoting good standards of revision...

Well now. It makes sense to make sure that products are made to good standards — think about how dangerous it could be if they weren't. We get into cars fairly confidently knowing that they've been put through lots of different safety tests — but it'd be a very different matter without these standards. Time for the next page...

KITEMARK and the Kitemark device are reproduced with kind permission of The British Standards Institution. They are registered trademarks in the United Kingdom and in certain other countries.

Mechanical Properties

To make sense of a material's properties, you've got to understand what the technical terms actually mean.

Compression and Tension — Squashing and Stretching

1) Objects can be loaded under compression or tension.

COMPRESSION
- Compression means that the object is being squashed.
- This bottle is under compression.

TENSION
- Tension means it's being stretched.
- This rope is under tension.

2) The maximum load that an object can withstand under tension (or compression) is called the tensile (or compressive) strength. If the load is bigger than this value, the object will break.

To Describe Materials Usefully You Need to Use the Right Words

STIFFNESS / FLEXIBILITY

If a material doesn't deform (change shape) much under a large load then it's stiff. If it changes shape easily it's flexible. A balance beam is fairly stiff, so it doesn't bend too much under a gymnast's weight.

Something can be made more rigid (stiffer) by using a different, stiffer material or by changing its shape (making it thicker, say) or structure (how it's built).

DURABILITY

A durable material is one that doesn't wear out too quickly. Most sports equipment needs to be durable because you don't want it to have to replace it after only a few uses.

The ropes used by rock climbers need to be durable, so they don't wear out too quickly due to forces acting on the rope.

DENSITY

A dense material has a large mass contained in a small volume. Most sports equipment is made from materials of low density, since you usually want it to be as light as possible.

You need a racing bike to be big enough for you but as light as possible (so you can go as fast as possible). Similarly, you'd want a lightweight tennis racket — it'd take a lot more effort to swing something really heavy.

TOUGHNESS / BRITTLENESS

A tough material can deform quite a lot without breaking. A brittle material breaks before it deforms very much at all.

Scuba diving fins need to bend a lot without breaking, so they're made of tough plastic.

HARDNESS

A hard material is resistant to scratching or indentation. A baseball is hard to resist the impact of the bat.

My head's pretty dense...

It's really important that you use the right words to describe properties of materials. It's easy to get confused, so make sure you know what's meant by stiff, flexible, tough, brittle, hard, dense and durable...

Unit 2: Topic 1 — Sports Equipment

Force-Extension Graphs

You need to know how to test the stiffness of a material. Luckily, this page tells you how...

You Can Use Force-Extension Graphs to Compare Stiffness...

1) To compare the stiffness (see p.42) of different materials, this is what you'd do:

   - Material under test
   - Paper marker — initially lined up with 0 cm on the ruler (when there was no load).
   - Ruler
   - Pulley
   - Original length — keep the same for all the materials to make it a fair test.
   - Load

2) Remember to wear safety specs and to keep your feet well away from the hanging loads.

3) Gradually increase the load on the material by adding weights, and measure the extension (total length − original length) of the material each time using a ruler, as shown above.

4) Plot a force-extension graph for each different material.

5) This graph shows the results of testing three different materials with increasingly heavy loads. The stiffest material is shown by the shallowest gradient.

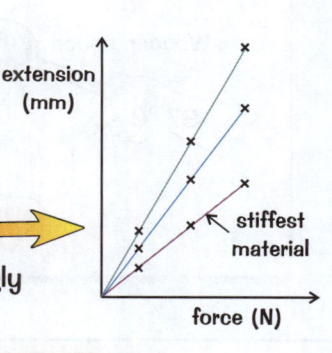

...and to Calculate the Energy Stored in a Stretched Sample

1) When a material is stretched, energy is transferred to the material. This energy is then stored in the stretched material.

2) You can calculate the energy stored in a stretched material using a force-extension graph — it's just the area under the graph.

3) If the area under the graph is a triangle, you can calculate the size of the area using the formula: $\dfrac{\text{Force (in N)} \times \text{Extension (in m)}}{2}$

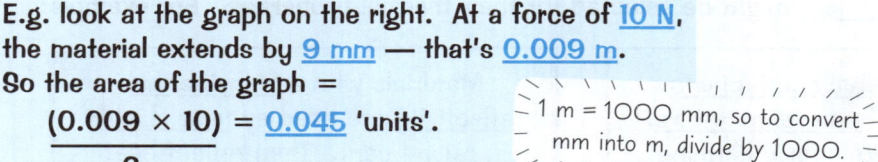

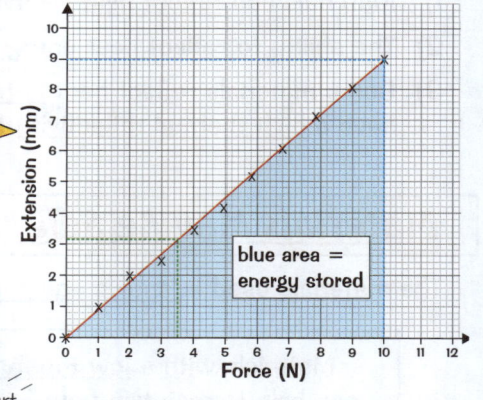

   E.g. look at the graph on the right. At a force of 10 N, the material extends by 9 mm — that's 0.009 m.
   So the area of the graph =
   $\dfrac{(0.009 \times 10)}{2}$ = 0.045 'units'.

   1 m = 1000 mm, so to convert mm into m, divide by 1000.

   The units for energy are joules (J). So the energy stored in this stretched material = 0.045 J.

4) You can also use a force-extension graph to predict how much a material will extend at a given force.

   E.g. say you wanted to predict how much the material in the graph will extend when you apply a force of 3.5 N. On the graph, draw a vertical line up from 3.5 N and a horizontal line across to the Extension axis (the green lines on the graph). This gives you a value of 3.2 mm. So you can predict that the material will extend by 3.2 mm.

I don't know about you, but I've found this page really stretching...

Make sure you know what experiment you'd do to test and compare the stiffness of materials in a laboratory. You also need to be able to use a force-extension graph to calculate the energy stored in a stretched sample.

Unit 2: Topic 1 — Sports Equipment

Thermal Properties

Sometimes, designers of sports equipment need to think about a material's thermal properties. Ooh err.

Thermal Conductivity is the Ability to Conduct Heat Energy

1) The ability to conduct heat energy is called thermal conductivity.
2) Materials with a high thermal conductivity (e.g. metals) conduct heat energy very quickly when there is a difference in temperature between one side of the material and the other. This means that heat energy flows through them easily.
3) Materials that have a very low thermal conductivity (e.g. air) are called thermal insulators — heat energy flows through them very slowly.
4) Sometimes two objects at the same temperature will feel as though they're at different temperatures. For example, a metal spoon will feel colder to the touch than a wooden spoon at the same temperature. This is because wood and metal have different thermal conductivities:

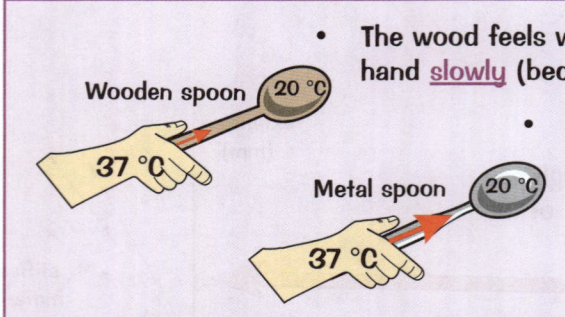

- The wood feels warm because heat flows from your hand slowly (because wood is a good insulator).
- The metal feels cold because heat flows from your hand quickly (because metal is a good conductor).
- The metal feels colder than the wood but it's actually at the same temperature. It's just that heat is flowing from your body at different rates.

Thermal Reflectivity is the Ability to Reflect Heat Energy

1) Materials can reflect heat — this means that heat energy hits them and bounces back.
2) The ability to reflect heat energy is called thermal reflectivity.
3) Some materials reflect heat better than others — light-coloured, shiny materials tend to have a high thermal reflectivity (i.e. they reflect a lot of the heat energy hitting them).

Materials May Be Selected for Their Thermal Properties

The materials used in sports equipment might be selected for their thermal properties. For example:

Materials with a low thermal conductivity can help to maintain your body temperature. They're often used to make sports clothing that needs to keep you warm, e.g. ski jackets.

Materials with a high thermal reflectivity are used as heat shields in racing cars. They reflect heat away from various car parts, helping to stop them from overheating.

Revision conductance — from the book to your head...

Compared to the previous page, this one's a doddle — no graphs, no calculations, just a bit of text to get your head around and some nice pictures of sporting activities. So there's really no excuse not to learn it.

Unit 2: Topic 1 — Sports Equipment

Material Properties

It's important that new sports products are made from suitable materials, and there's plenty of choice...

Designers Need to Use Criteria to Select the Right Materials

1) Designers need to think carefully about what materials they could use to make a product.
2) The materials they choose need to meet certain criteria to make them suitable for the product. The criteria a designer needs to consider include: a material's properties (see below), its durability (see page 42), its cost, its environmental impact and its aesthetic appeal (how attractive the material is). Here's an example:

> Racing bikes need to be light and strong. The best materials tend to be very expensive, so manufacturers need to choose the material very carefully if they want to sell the bikes in any great quantity.

Different Materials are Suited to Different Jobs

What materials are used for depends on their properties.

Different Metals Have Different Properties...

...but, generally speaking, most metals are:

1) MALLEABLE — they can be hammered or rolled into flat sheets or pipes.
2) GOOD CONDUCTORS of heat and electricity.
3) DUCTILE — they can be drawn into wires.
4) SHINY
5) STIFF

> Metals are used to make running spikes and javelin points. They're also used in electrical systems in racing cars.

Polymers Have Many Useful Properties

Polymers include nylon, polythene and PVC.

1) Polymers are INSULATORS of heat and electricity.
2) They're often FLEXIBLE — they can be bent without breaking.
3) They're EASILY MOULDED — they can be used to manufacture equipment with almost any shape.

> Polymers are used to make things like crash helmets and kayaks.

Polymers are just plastics, made by joining loads of little molecules together in long chains.

Ceramics are Stiff but Brittle

Ceramics include glass, porcelain and bone china (for posh tea cups). They are:

1) INSULATORS of heat and electricity.
2) BRITTLE — they aren't very flexible and break easily.
3) STIFF

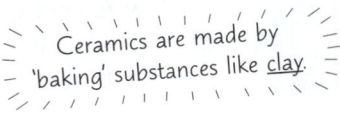

> Ceramics are used for brakes and parts of spark plugs in racing cars.

Ceramics are made by 'baking' substances like clay.

My Mum keeps telling me to learn some uses of iron...

It's important to take a material's properties into account when designing things — you wouldn't want to use a brittle ceramic to make a cricket bat, for example. But you also need to think about things like cost.

Unit 2: Topic 1 — Sports Equipment

More on Material Properties

Some products need a combination of different properties. That's where composites come in...

Composites are Made of Different Materials

Composites are made of one material embedded in another. The properties of a composite depend on the properties of the materials it is made from. For example:

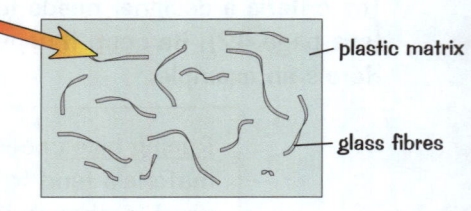

1) **FIBREGLASS** (or Glass Reinforced Plastic — GRP) consists of fibres of glass embedded in a matrix of plastic. It has a low density (like plastic) but is very strong (like glass). These properties mean fibreglass is used for things like skis, boats and surfboards.

2) **CONCRETE** is made from aggregate (a mixture of sand and gravel) embedded in cement. It has a high compressive strength (see p.42). This makes it ideal for use as a building material, e.g. in skate parks.

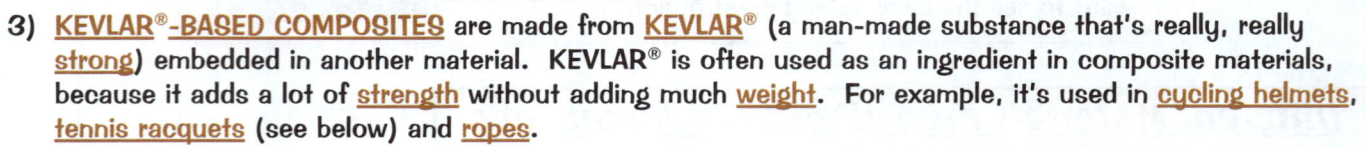

3) **KEVLAR®-BASED COMPOSITES** are made from KEVLAR® (a man-made substance that's really, really strong) embedded in another material. KEVLAR® is often used as an ingredient in composite materials, because it adds a lot of strength without adding much weight. For example, it's used in cycling helmets, tennis racquets (see below) and ropes.

The Development of New Materials Has Changed Sports Equipment

Sports equipment has changed over time due to the development of new materials. This has lead to improvements in sporting performance. You need to learn these two examples:

1) **Tennis racquets** — these used to be made of wood, which made them quite heavy. Now they're made from new lighter, stronger materials, such as graphite mixed with fibreglass or KEVLAR®. This allows tennis players to hit the ball with more force.

2) **Golf balls** — these were originally made from wood, then from leather pouches filled with feathers, then from rubber. They're now made from layers of lightweight plastic with a dimpled outer layer — this allows the ball to travel a long way.

You Need to Be Able to Interpret Information about Materials

In the exam they might ask you to interpret information about the properties of materials and assess the suitability of these materials for different types of sports equipment.

Type of material	Properties
Aluminium	Strong and hard, lightweight for a metal
Neoprene (a polymer)	Flexible, low thermal conductivity
Glass (a ceramic)	Stiff, low thermal conductivity
Plasticised polymer	Flexible and light, can be easily moulded

Examples: 
1) A fencing sword should be strong and hard enough to withstand clashes in a sword fight, and lightweight enough to be handled easily — aluminium is a good choice.

2) A scuba diving suit should be flexible to allow for comfortable movement, and provide enough insulation to keep divers warm — neoprene is a good choice.

Statues of football legends — got to choose the Best material...

In the exam, don't panic if you're asked to interpret information about a material you've never heard of before. You'll be given all the information you need to answer the question. Just make sure you read it through carefully.

Unit 2: Topic 1 — Sports Equipment

Revision Summary

You really shouldn't skip these questions. What's the point in reading the entire section if you're not going to check whether you really know it all? When it comes to the exam, you'll be glad you did.

1) Give two skills material scientists need to do their job.
2) Explain why it's important that products are made to a good standard.
3) Give the name of an organisation that sets product standards.
4) Why are products made with a safety margin?
5) What do the terms compression and tension mean?
6) Give one way in which you could make something more rigid (stiff).
7) What does it mean when a material is described as durable?
8) Explain using a diagram how you'd test the stiffness of a material.
9)* Which material, A, B or C, shown on the force-extension graph is the stiffest?
10) Explain what is meant by the terms:
    a) thermal conductivity,
    b) thermal reflectivity.
11) Explain why ski jackets are often made from materials with low thermal conductivity.
12) Suggest some criteria that designers think about when considering materials for their products.
13) Describe three properties of:
    a) metals,
    b) polymers,
    c) ceramics.
14) What is a composite material?
15) Give an example of a composite material.
16) a) Describe how the development of new materials has led to changes in tennis racquets over time.
    b) Explain how these changes have affected the performance of tennis players.
17)*Choosing from the materials in the table, which would you use for:
    a) Body armour for mountain biking?
    b) Clothing for riding a motorcycle?
    c) Making a high-performance bicycle?

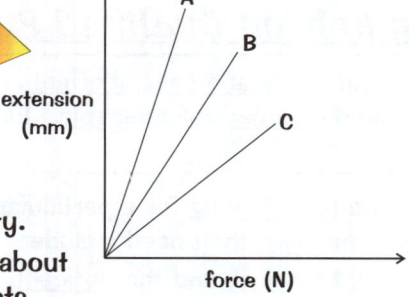

Material	Properties
A	Low density, strong, lightweight, expensive
B	Lightweight, hard, strong, water-resistant
C	Elastic, lightweight, durable, flexible
D	Tough, strong, durable, flexible

*Answers on p.108.

Unit 2: Topic 1 — Sports Equipment

Unit 2: Topic 2 — Stage and Screen

Managing Stage and Screen

It's time to learn about stage and screen, dahlings... This topic is about how sound and lighting are used in stage and screen. First up, the people who set-up and use these sound and lighting effects. Break a leg, folks.

Sound and Light Effects Are Used By Lots of Different Organisations

Sound and light effects are used to enhance (improve) stage and screen performances. Below are some examples of organisations that use sound and light effects to improve the experience for their audience.

- Theatres 
- Music Venues 
- Film and TV Companies

The Stage and Screen Rely on Qualified Practitioners

Light engineers, sound engineers and visual and special effects experts play an important part in stage and screen. They're specially trained and qualified for their role. Each role requires scientific and technical skills.

Light Engineer

Light engineers work to create the best lighting for a particular situation. They use different materials and sources of light to do this. The skills they need include:
1) A good knowledge of light, light sources and the optical properties of different materials (see p.50).
2) The ability to set-up lighting equipment and use filters to produce different colours (see p.49).
3) The creativity to plan and carry out how the lighting should look — to help "set a scene".

Sound Engineer

Sound engineers make sure sound can be heard, is a good quality and safe. The skills they need include:
1) A good knowledge of sound and how it works (see p.53).
2) An understanding of the decibel scale — making sure sound stays within a safe level (see p.53).
3) The ability to set-up equipment correctly to get the best sound possible (see p.55).
4) Knowledge of the materials that absorb and reflect sound — to get the venue acoustics right (p.54).

Visual and Special Effects Experts

Visual and special effects experts are in charge of any special effects in a production. They sometimes specialise in one particular area, e.g. electronics or explosives. The skills they need include:
1) A good knowledge of materials and techniques to produce special effects.
2) The ability to design, make, use and maintain any equipment.

Engineers and Special Effects Experts Have Regulations to Follow

Light engineers, sound engineers and visual and special effects experts must follow regulations to keep themselves and the people they work with safe and well. For example:
1) They must regularly maintain any equipment and always use it correctly and safely.
2) They must know about the dangers of light (see page 49), sound (see page 53) and special effects (e.g. explosives), and work to reduce any risks.

Lights, camera, revision...

I don't know about you, but I reckon this stuff is pretty interesting. Light and sound engineers are very clever bunnies — they use their skills to make the lighting or sound the best it can be. Without them, plays, TV shows, films and concerts wouldn't be half as good. And life without special effects experts doesn't bear thinking about...

Unit 2: Topic 2 — Stage and Screen

Managing Light

A variety of light sources are used in films and on stage...

Different Light Sources are Used for Different Things

The following are all types of light sources that might be used on stage or when making films or TV shows:

Sunlight

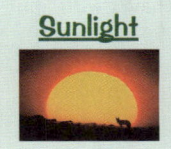

Incandescent lamps — Light bulbs with a wire inside that glows when it gets hot.

Fluorescent lamps — Low-energy light bulbs.

Lasers — Light from a laser is a single colour.

Some Light Sources Give Out Unwanted Radiation

Some light sources produce infra-red (IR) or ultra-violet (UV) radiation. These can cause problems:

IR RADIATION
1) IR radiation is emitted (given out) by all hot objects. The hotter the object, the more IR radiation it emits.
2) Objects can absorb (take in) IR radiation too.
3) Light sources, e.g. bulbs, get very hot when they're used and so give out IR radiation.
4) This IR radiation causes heating.

UV RADIATION
1) UV radiation is given out by the Sun.
2) Other light sources, e.g. fluorescent lamps, can also give out UV radiation.
3) UV rays can cause skin cancer.

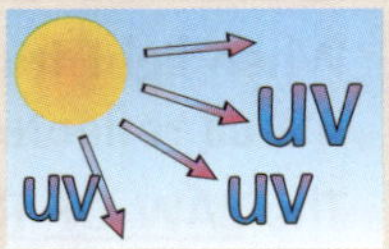

Filters can be Used to Remove Harmful IR and UV Radiation...

Filters can be used to absorb UV and IR radiation. They're usually made of plastic or glass, e.g. the windows of a building filter out some of the UV radiation from the Sun. IR filters are often used in devices which have incandescent lamps in them, e.g. projectors. These IR filters let light through but absorb some of the IR.

...and They can Also be Used to Absorb and Transmit Colours

All colours of light can be made using a mix of red, green and/or blue light.

1) Red, green and blue light mix to make white light.
2) Red and green light mix to make yellow.
3) Red and blue light mix to make magenta.
4) Blue and green light mix to make cyan. 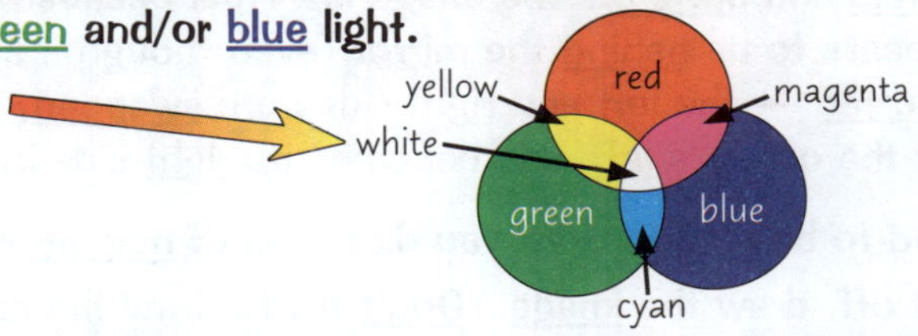
5) Filters change the colour of a light source by absorbing some colours and transmitting (letting through) others. Here's what happens if you use different colour filters on white light:

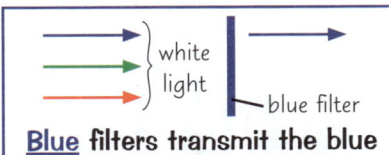

Blue filters transmit the blue light and absorb the others.

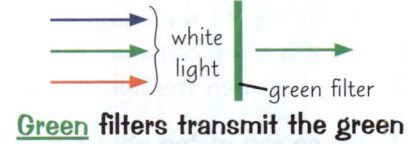

Green filters transmit the green light and absorb the others.

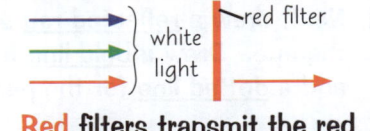

Red filters transmit the red light and absorb the others.

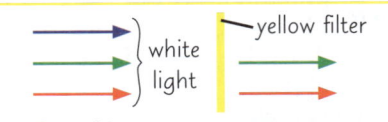

Yellow filters transmit green and red light, and absorb blue light.

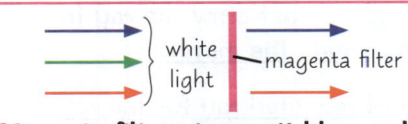

Magenta filters transmit blue and red light, and absorb green light.

Cyan filters transmit blue and green light, and absorb red light.

Absorb and transmit this information...

Wow, that was a colour blast. If your eyes haven't been damaged by the brightness, it's time for the next page...

Unit 2: Topic 2 — Stage and Screen

Optical Properties

Lighting effects in stage and screen can be created by making use of the optical properties of materials.

You Need to Know How to Describe Optical Properties

1) **Transparent** — a material is transparent if you can see through it clearly.
2) **Reflective** — a material is very reflective if most of the light that falls on it reflects (bounces) back off (see below).
3) **Translucent** — light can pass through the material but you can't see through it clearly. Frosted glass (like the glass used in bathroom windows) is translucent.
4) **Opaque** — a material is opaque if light can't pass through it.
5) **Refractive** — refraction is the bending of a light ray when it passes from one medium (material) to another at an angle. Lenses work by refraction (see p.51).

The optical property of something just means how it behaves with light.

Know How Light Reflects off a Mirror...

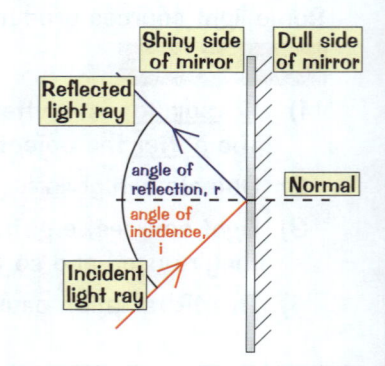

1) When light travelling in the same direction reflects from a mirror, then it's all reflected at the same angle and you get a clear reflection.
2) The LAW OF REFLECTION applies to every reflected ray:

Angle of INCIDENCE = Angle of REFLECTION

Note that these two angles are ALWAYS defined between the ray itself and the NORMAL (the dotted line shown on the diagram on the right). Don't ever label them as the angle between the ray and the surface of the mirror.

...and How to Draw a Ray Diagram for an Image in a Plane Mirror

An image of an object can be formed using a plane (flat) mirror. When this happens, the image is always...

1) The same size as the object.
2) As far behind the mirror as the object is in front.
3) Virtual and upright. The image is virtual because the object appears to be behind the mirror (even though it's not).
4) Inverted — the left and right sides are swapped, i.e. the object's left side becomes its right side in the image.

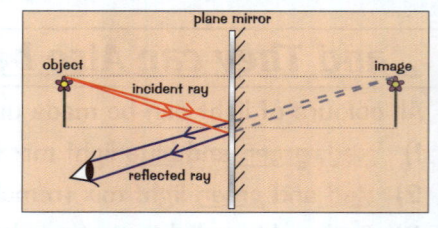

You need to be able to draw ray diagrams of how an image of a distant object is formed in a plane mirror:

1) First off, draw the image. Don't try to draw the rays first. Follow the rules in the above box — the image is the same size, and it's as far behind the mirror as the object is in front.

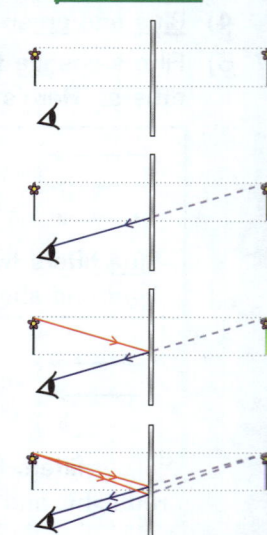

2) Next, draw a reflected ray going from the top of the image to the top of the eye. Draw a bold line for the part of the ray between the mirror and eye, and a dotted line for the part of the ray between the mirror and image.

3) Now draw the incident ray going from the top of the object to the mirror. The incident and reflected rays follow the law of reflection — but you don't actually have to measure any angles. Just draw the ray from the object to the point where the reflected ray meets the mirror.

4) Now you have an incident ray and reflected ray for the top of the image. Do steps 2 and 3 again for the bottom of the eye — a reflected ray going from the image to the bottom of the eye, then an incident ray from the object to the mirror.

Plane mirrors — what pilots use to look behind them...

Make sure you can draw clear ray diagrams and you'll be well on your way to picking up lotsa marks in the exam.

Unit 2: Topic 2 — Stage and Screen

Lenses

A lens is just a piece of glass (or sometimes plastic) that's been shaped so as to focus light. All lenses change the direction of light rays by refraction. They can be used in lights to create lighting effects.

Fatter Lenses Bend Light More

1) Lenses are useful because they refract (bend) rays of light.
2) There are two types of lenses you need to know about — converging and diverging.
3) For both types of lens, the fatter the lens, the more it bends the light.

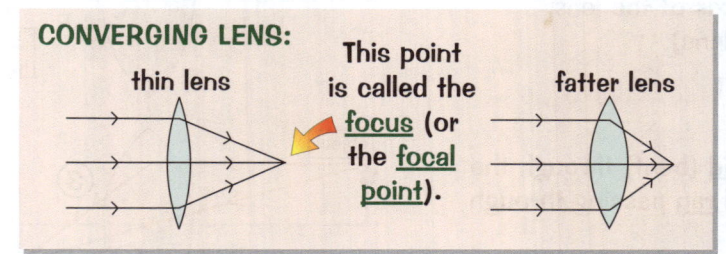

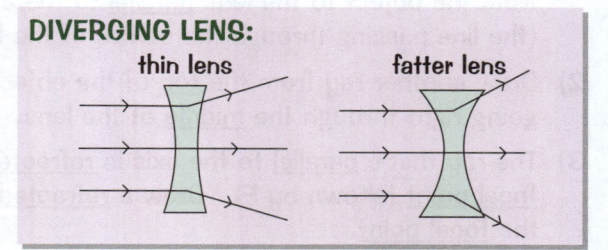

CONVERGING LENS: thin lens — This point is called the focus (or the focal point) — fatter lens

DIVERGING LENS: thin lens — fatter lens

Converging Lenses Focus Parallel Rays Onto a Point

You can see objects because light reflects off them and reaches your eyes.

1) Light rays that reach your eyes from a point on a distant object are parallel to each other.
2) A converging lens brings these parallel rays together at a point.
3) The fatter or more curved a lens is, the closer the image will be formed to the lens.

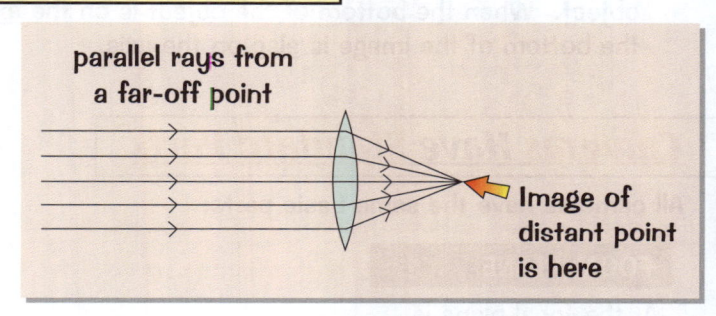

parallel rays from a far-off point — Image of distant point is here

Diverging Lenses Focus Parallel Rays Away From a Point

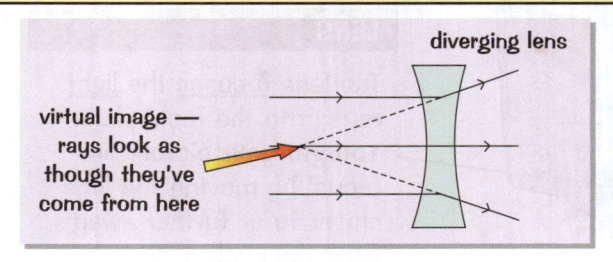

virtual image — rays look as though they've come from here — diverging lens

1) A diverging lens refracts parallel light rays away from each other.
2) The refracted rays look as if they've come from a point close to the lens — but they haven't really.
3) You get a virtual image at the point they seem to have come from.

The Lens Material Affects How Much it Bends Light

1) Different materials bend light different amounts when light enters them.
2) For example, light slows down more in glass than it does in Perspex® (a type of plastic).
3) So if you have two lenses that are the same shape and size, but one's made from Perspex® and the other from glass, then the glass lens will refract (bend) light entering it more than the Perspex® lens.

Don't lose your focus — learn this stuff...

Make sure you know what converging and diverging lenses do. They both bend parallel rays, but converging lenses bring rays together at a point, whereas diverging lenses bend rays away from each other. So there you go.

Unit 2: Topic 2 — Stage and Screen

Lenses and Images

You'll find lenses in cameras and glasses (the ones that sit on your nose). The lenses are used to take light from a distant object and to form an image of that object.

Draw a Ray Diagram for an Image Through a Converging Lens

You need to be able to draw a ray diagram to show how an image of a distant object is formed by a converging lens. Here's how you do it:

1) Pick a point on the top of the object. Draw a ray going from the object to the lens parallel to the axis of the lens (the line passing through the centre of the lens).

2) Draw another ray from the top of the object going right through the middle of the lens.

3) The ray that's parallel to the axis is refracted (bent) through the focal point (shown by F). Draw a refracted ray passing through the focal point.

4) The ray passing through the middle of the lens doesn't bend.

5) Mark where the rays meet. That's the top of the image.

6) Repeat the process for a point on the bottom of the object. When the bottom of the object is on the axis, the bottom of the image is also on the axis.

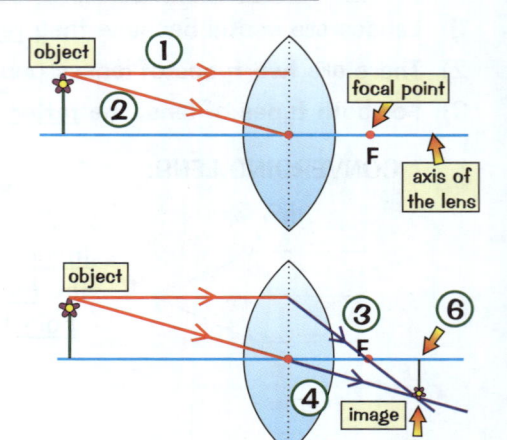

If there was no focal point marked, you'd still bend the parallel ray in the lens — you'd just have to make sure it meets your other line at a point somewhere.

Cameras Have Standard Parts

All cameras have the same basic parts:

FOCAL PLANE
At the focal plane is the camera film or a CCD (if it's a digital camera).

SHUTTER
The shutter is a flap covering the film that opens for a very short time when you take a picture.

APERTURE
The aperture is an adjustable hole — you change its size to allow the right amount of light in. It does the same thing as the pupil in your eye.

VIEWFINDER
The viewfinder is a lens that you look through to see what the picture will be like. Some digital cameras don't have one of these — you look at a small screen instead.

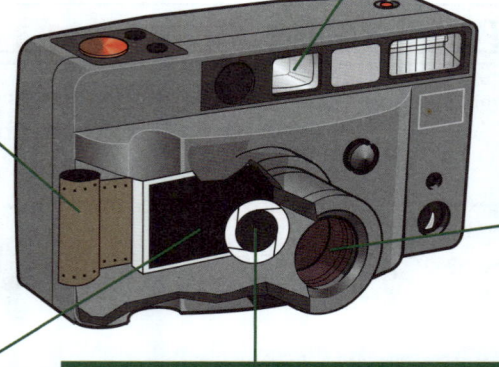

LENS
The lens focuses the light rays onto the focal plane. You get your picture 'in focus' by moving the lens closer to or further away from the back of the camera.

Smile and say cheese...

In the exam, you could be given a picture of a camera and be asked to label all the parts. So make sure you can. Don't panic though — it's all on this page, so just take your time and learn it bit by bit. And don't be put off if the picture of the camera looks more modern than the one above. I borrowed the one above off my Nana.

Unit 2: Topic 2 — Stage and Screen

Acoustic Properties

To do their job, sound engineers need to have a really good understanding of acoustic (sound) properties. And so do you, so read on...

Pitch and Loudness Depend on the Vibrations Causing Them

1) Sounds are caused when objects vibrate at certain frequencies.
2) The pitch of the sound depends on the frequency of vibration (the number of vibrations per second). You can produce a high-pitched sound by making something vibrate very quickly.

> For example, guitar players make different notes by pressing the strings against the neck of the guitar — this effectively shortens the string. Shorter strings vibrate faster than longer ones, and these faster vibrations produce higher-pitched notes.

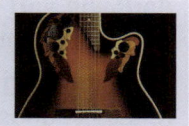

3) The loudness (or intensity) of a sound depends on the amplitude of the vibrations (how far the object moves backwards and forwards or side to side). The bigger the vibrations the louder the sound.

> For example, if you hit a cymbal hard, it moves a long way up and down — it vibrates with a large amplitude. This creates a loud sound. If you give the cymbal a gentle tap, it vibrates with a small amplitude. This makes a quiet sound.

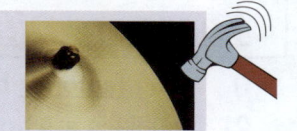

The Decibel Scale Measures Loudness

1) You can measure the intensity (loudness) of a sound using the decibel (dB) scale.
2) The decibel scale is not a linear scale. An increase of 10 dB in intensity means a doubling in loudness. So, if the intensity increases by 20 dB the sound will be four times louder.
3) If you listen to loud sounds for a long time you can damage your ears. This might result in permanent hearing loss or tinnitus – a 'ringing' in your ear. MP3 players sometimes have limiters which stop the volume reaching damaging levels.

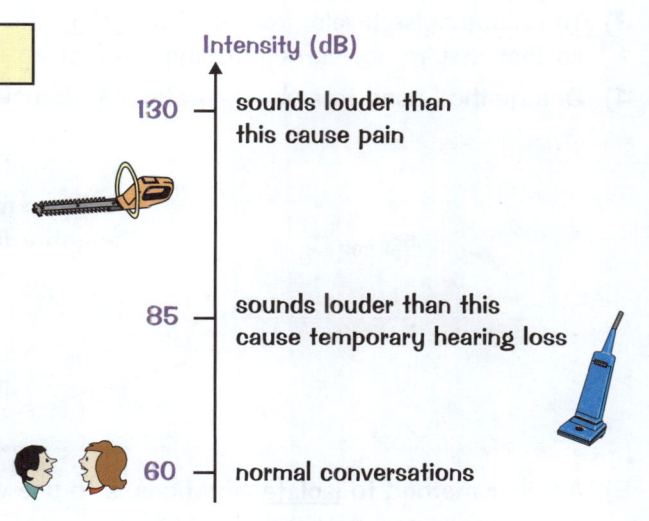

Intensity (dB)
- 130 — sounds louder than this cause pain
- 85 — sounds louder than this cause temporary hearing loss
- 60 — normal conversations

Ears Can Hear Sounds of Many Frequencies

1) Your ears are more sensitive to some frequencies of sound than others — some frequencies have to be quite intense before you can hear them at all.
2) The ear is most sensitive at around 2000 Hz (vibrations per second). You can hear very quiet sounds at this frequency — and sounds at 2000 Hz seem louder than sounds at other frequencies even if they have the same intensity. (Fire alarms are usually set at 2000 Hz so that almost everybody will be able to hear them.)
3) The ear just can't hear sounds with too high or too low a frequency — that's why dog whistles are silent to humans.

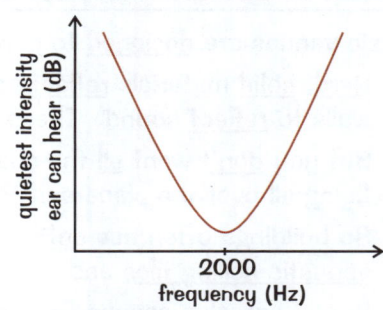

Acoustics — hmm, I prefer the electric guitar...

It's all about frequency and amplitude here. These two things affect the pitch and the loudness of a sound. The higher the frequency of the vibration, the higher pitched the sound will be. The higher the amplitude of the vibration, the louder the sound will be. And, remember, sounds above a certain loudness can damage your hearing.

Unit 2: Topic 2 — Stage and Screen

Controlling Sound

Now you know how dangerous sound can be, it's time to learn how to control it. And no, it doesn't involve drugs and a cage. Sound needs to be controlled not only in very loud places, but in normal buildings too.

Sound Needs to be Controlled in Buildings

1) Too much noise can be a real problem, particularly for people who live in blocks of flats or in terraced houses. But there are ways to design buildings or decorate rooms so they're quieter.
2) To reduce noise levels, you need to absorb sounds generated inside and reflect sounds made outside.
3) Anything soft will absorb sounds. For example, you might put underlay beneath carpets or laminate flooring. Special acoustic ceiling tiles can help reduce the noise from above or below a room.
4) Anything hard with a flat surface will reflect sounds. For example, windows are hard, flat surfaces that reflect sounds like traffic noise, stopping most of it from entering your house. Double-glazing uses two layers of glass and so reflects even more sound.

There are Different Ways to Isolate Vibrations

1) Many factories have lots of very noisy machinery.
2) Machines are noisy because they're vibrating — and these vibrations may be carried around a factory, since factory buildings are usually rigid structures — they don't absorb vibrations much.
3) To reduce noise levels, you need to isolate the machines' vibrations so that they're not carried around the factory.
4) One method used to isolate vibrations is to use a supporting floor with fluid-filled dampers.

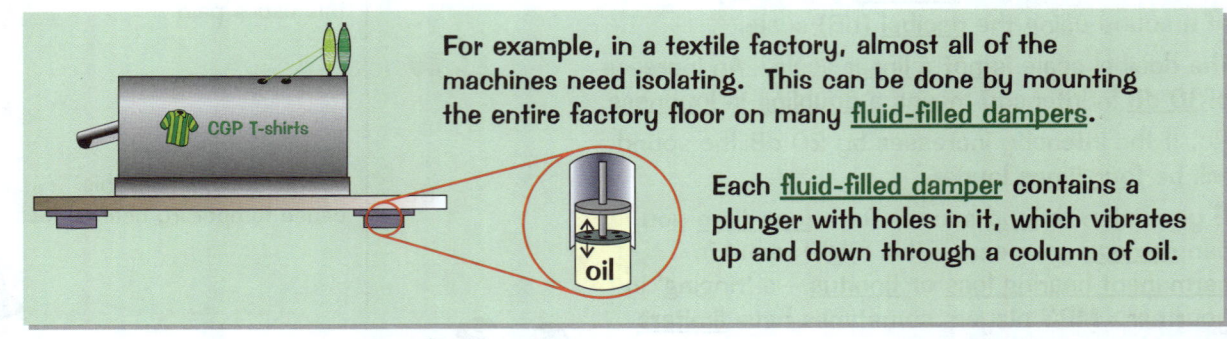

For example, in a textile factory, almost all of the machines need isolating. This can be done by mounting the entire factory floor on many fluid-filled dampers.

Each fluid-filled damper contains a plunger with holes in it, which vibrates up and down through a column of oil.

5) Another method to isolate vibrations is to use wire suspensions — this involves equipment being mounted on a surface and suspended using wires.
6) Machinery can also be mounted on rubber pads.

The Acoustics in a Music Venue can be Controlled Using Materials

Music venues are designed to control the acoustics, using reflective and absorbing surfaces.

1) Hard, solid materials reflect sound. So, a venue might have double-glazed windows and concrete or brick walls to reflect sound. These help sound-proof a room — it's harder for sound to escape or get in.
2) But you don't want all the sound from inside a venue to be reflected — there would be echoes flying all over the place and the sound would be terrible.
3) So buildings often use soft materials too. A venue might have fabric panels on the wall, acoustic ceiling tiles and underlay (see above).
4) Sound can also escape from any gaps in a room or building — so a music venue might have thicker doors.

Underlay, underlay, ariba, ariba...

Make sure you can name at least two ways in which sound can be reflected or absorbed in a normal building or in a music venue. Test yourself by covering up the page and scribbling down everything you can remember.

Unit 2: Topic 2 — Stage and Screen

Managing Sound and Electrics

In a performance venue, sound is usually managed using a sound system. You need to be able to describe how a simple sound system works. And how to avoid howl — this has nothing to do with a full moon.

A Simple Sound System Can Be Made With Three Things

1) Sound systems can be used to make a sound louder in a venue. For example, someone talking to a large group of people might use a sound system so more people can hear what they're saying.

2) A simple sound system is made up of:

A microphone	An amplifier	A loudspeaker
What someone talks or sings into. The sound is converted to an electrical signal.	The amplifier takes the signal from the microphone and makes it more powerful.	The loudspeaker turns the signal from the amplifier into sound — and we can hear the person talking or singing.

3) Sometimes you might hear a sound system give out a loud noise like a howl — this is called feedback.

4) Feedback happens when sound from the loudspeaker gets picked up by the microphone, is re-amplified and comes back out again through the loudspeakers. This will carry on in a loop until the microphone or speakers are moved.

5) There are a few tricks you can use when setting up a sound system to avoid getting feedback. For example, the speakers should be put **IN FRONT** of the microphone (not behind it) and should **POINT AWAY** from the microphone. This helps stop the microphone picking up any sound from the speakers.

You Need to Know about Circuits for Lights in Venues

Lighting in indoor venues needs to be easy to control. You want to be able to turn lights on and off, and change their brightness. To do this you need switches and dimmers in the electrical circuits for the lights.

1) Switches in an electrical circuit can be open or closed.
2) If the switch is open, no current will flow and so any lamps in the circuit won't light up.
3) If the switch is closed, current will flow and the lamp will light up.
4) In an electrical circuit, a variable resistor can be used as a dimmer.
5) The variable resistor is used to change the resistance in the circuit — the greater the resistance, the less current will flow and the dimmer the lamp will be.
6) Below are two examples of circuit diagrams that have lamps in them:

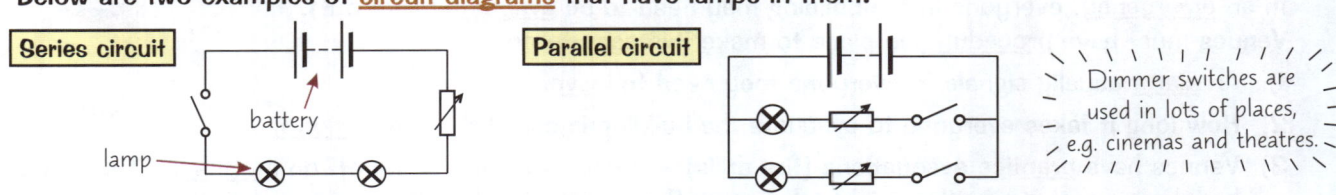

Dimmer switches are used in lots of places, e.g. cinemas and theatres.

7) In the series circuit above, the switch, variable resistor and lamps are all in a loop. This means the switch and variable resistor affect both lamps at the same time, e.g. closing the switch turns both lamps on. If one lamp breaks, the circuit will be broken and the other lamp won't work.

8) In the parallel circuit above, each lamp is connected separately to the battery with a switch and variable resistor. This means they can be dimmed or turned off individually. Also, if one lamp breaks or is removed, the other lamp will be unaffected.

Talent show put down #72: "Is that howl — or your singing..."

Make sure you know how to set-up a sound system to avoid howl. Or howl hunt you down. You have been warned.

Unit 2: Topic 2 — Stage and Screen

Managing Indoor Venues

When an indoor venue is being designed, you have to bear in mind health and safety. We aren't just talking emergency exits, there's all sorts of stuff you need to consider. But first up, schematic drawings...

Schematic Drawings Can Show The Main Features of a Venue

Schematic drawings are diagrams that show the main features of something.

1) Schematic drawings don't need to look realistic — they're more like a sketch. They're usually made up of lines and symbols.
2) Circuit diagrams (see p.55) are examples of schematic drawings — circuits don't look like that in real life, but the diagrams show all the important stuff you need to see in a simple way.
3) You need to be able to interpret simple schematic drawings of a performance venue (e.g. a theatre) and point out the main sources of heat and ventilation (how air can get in and out of the room).
4) Take a look at the schematic drawing below of part of the Chorley National Indoor Arena:

When drawing schematics, you can ignore the things you're not interested in.

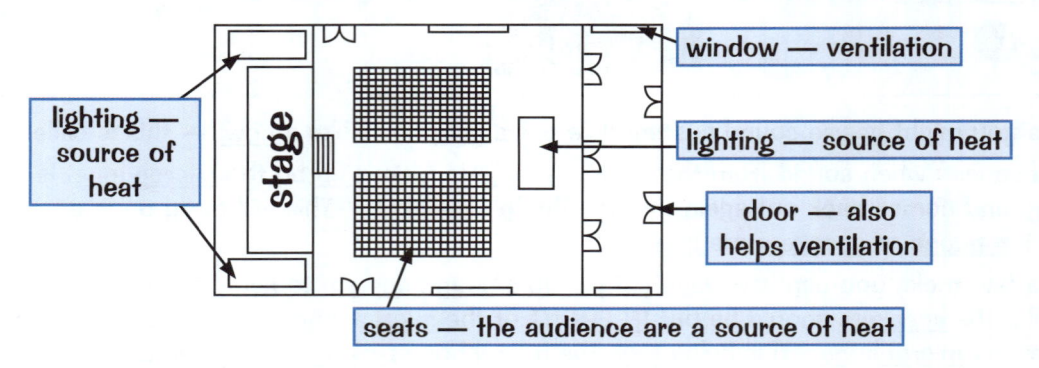

- lighting — source of heat
- stage
- window — ventilation
- lighting — source of heat
- door — also helps ventilation
- seats — the audience are a source of heat

Some Health and Safety Rules Have To Be Followed By Law

In performance venues, there are usually lots of people all in one place. These venues have to follow statutory health and safety rules, in order to keep everyone safe and to get everyone out of the building quickly if there is an emergency. Here are some rules you need to know about:

If something is statutory it means you have to do it by law. Them's the rules.

VENUES MUST HAVE:

1) Emergency exits that are clearly signed and lit up.
2) Emergency lighting — in case the mains power fails.
3) Fireproof curtains and doors — this is to stop fire spreading.

VENUES MUST HAVE PROCEDURES:

In an emergency, everyone in the building may need to be evacuated (got out). Venues must have procedures in place to make this easy to do.

1) An alarm usually signals to everyone they need to leave.
2) How long it takes everyone to evacuate the building is called the evacuation time.
3) Venues have practice evacuations (fire drills) — where an alarm is set off on purpose. This shows how long a real evacuation might take — staff can then decide if there are ways to improve this.
4) Practice evacuations can also show problems with people flow — how people move around a building. If too many people try to leave by one exit it causes problems and slows down the evacuation.
5) More exits might be put in or people might be told to leave by certain exits. For example, people sitting to the left of the stage in a theatre will be told to leave by the emergency exits on the left.

This is not a drill...

Next time you're in a venue, try and spot all the sources of heat and ventilation. You only need to make rough notes — then e-mail your three best friends with your observations. They'll definitely appreciate the information.

Unit 2: Topic 2 — Stage and Screen

Revision Summary

Well the curtain has closed on this topic. And you were fabulous at revising this stuff, you really were, darling. You stole the show... Actually, the show isn't quite over just yet. It's time to crack on with these questions and check that everything you've just learnt hasn't fallen out of your head. It can happen, you know.

1) Name three types of organisation that might use sound and light effects.
2) a) Name a qualified practitioner who works with sound.
   b) Describe the role of this qualified practitioner.
3) Name four sources of light used in stage and screen.
4) Give one problem the IR radiation released from light sources causes.
5) Explain why the unwanted UV radiation from light sources can be dangerous.
6) Suggest one way you can reduce the risks of using light sources which release unwanted IR and UV radiation.
7) What colour light does a blue filter transmit?
8) Suggest how you could make white light appear magenta.
9) Define the following words:
   a) transparent
   b) translucent
   c) opaque
10) Sketch a ray diagram to show how an image is formed in a plane mirror.
11) What happens to parallel rays which hit a converging lens?
12) What happens to parallel rays which hit a diverging lens?
13) Will light refract more through a glass or Perspex® lens?
14) Sketch a ray diagram to show how an image of a distant object is formed by a converging lens.
15) Name five basic parts that all cameras have.
16) What does the pitch of a sound depend on?
17) What is the scale used to describe sound intensity?
18) What is the approximate sound level of normal conversations?
19) At what frequency is the ear most sensitive to sound?
20) Give two ways used to isolate vibrations.
21) Suggest one material you might find in a music venue which reflects sound.
22) Suggest one method used at a music venue to absorb sound.
23) A simple sound system is made up of a microphone, amplifier and loudspeaker.
    a) What causes howl in a sound system?
    b) Suggest one way you could set-up the equipment to avoid howl.
24) What can a variable resistor be used as in an electrical circuit containing a lamp?
25) Suggest one source of heat that might be found in a music venue.
26) Why must performance venues have emergency lighting?
27) Explain what is meant by the 'evacuation time' for a building.

Unit 2: Topic 2 — Stage and Screen

Unit 2: Topic 3 — Agriculture and Biotechnology

Agriculture in the UK

A lot of the food we eat in the UK is produced by British farmers. There are different types of farming, such as arable or dairy farming. Yee haarr.

Agriculture is Growing Living Organisms for Their Products

Agriculture is the posh word for farming. There are different types of agriculture, for example:

Arable Farming

Arable farming involves growing crops for humans and animals to eat. Many of the crops grown are used to make other food products. For example:
- Wheat is used to produce flour for making bread (see page 62).
- Barley is used in the production of beer.

Dairy Farming

Dairy cattle produce milk, which is also used to make milk products such as cheese and yoghurt (see page 69).

Biotechnology Can be Used in Food Production

Biotechnology includes the use of microorganisms during food processing and production, see pages 67-72. For example:

1) Yeast is used in the brewing and wine industries to make alcohol.
2) Yeast is also used in bread making.
3) Bacteria are used to turn milk into cheese and yoghurt.
4) Fungi make mycoprotein — meat substitutes for vegetarians.

You Might Have to Interpret Data on This Stuff in the Exam...

You may be asked to interpret some data on agriculture and the food industry in the exam. So here's some data on arable farming in the UK. The table shows the area of land used for growing three different crops over three years.

	Thousand Hectares		
	Dec '04	Dec '05	Dec '06
Wheat	1834	1771	1850
Barley	391	393	389
Oats	63	87	106

© Crown Copyright March 2007
Department for Environment, Food & Rural Affairs, Foss House, 1-2 Peasholme Green, York YO1 7PX

From the table you can see that:
1) Wheat covers the largest area of land every year.
2) The area of land used for barley has stayed fairly constant.
3) The area of land used for growing oats has increased.

How does a dairy farmer count his cows...?*

Data on agriculture could come in many different forms — like articles, flow charts, diagrams and tables (like the one above). There's lots more data interpretation still to come in this section, you lucky, lucky people.

*With a cowculator.

Regulating Agriculture and Food

You've learnt a bit about the food, glorious food, that's grown in this country, but how does it get from the field to your kitchen — the chain of food production, that's how.

The Chain of Food Production — From The Farm to Your Fridge

The chain of food production includes every stage from growing the food to getting it to your home.

1) **GROWING** — crops and animals are grown on farms. Microorganisms are grown in fermenters in factories.

2) **TRANSPORTING** — the harvested product may be transported from the farm to another site for processing.

3) **PROCESSING** — the product may be processed, e.g. milk needs to be pasteurised. Microorganisms can be used in processing.

There's more about pasteurising milk on page 66.

4) **STORING** — if not all the processed product is required immediately, some of it will have to be stored until it is needed, e.g. supermarket chains store goods at large distribution centres before they're taken to individual supermarkets.

5) **DELIVERING** — finally the processed product will be delivered to the shops for you to buy and take back to your home.

Agriculture and Food Production is Regulated

Agriculture is regulated for three important reasons:

1) Health and safety of workers — farms and factories involved in food production are checked regularly to make sure they're working in a safe manner and are looking after the health of the workers.
2) Health and safety of customers — places involved in food production are checked to make sure they're hygienic (clean) and the food produced there is of a good quality.
3) Animal welfare — by law animals must be treated humanely, including on the farm, at market, during transportation and at slaughter.

Chocolate to mouth — my favourite food chain...

The term 'chain of food production' is used in agriculture and food production industries to describe the stages involved in food production. Thankfully there are regulations to make sure we get good quality food that isn't going to make us ill. And the workers and animals involved are well looked after too, so everyone's happy.

Unit 2: Topic 3 — Agriculture and Biotechnology

More on Regulating Agriculture and Food

Food products must be tested to make sure that they're safe to eat and that they're good quality. There's a whole team of people to check that everyone involved in food production follows health and safety rules.

Enforcement Officers Monitor the Food Chain

Enforcement officers work for many different organisations. They're responsible for making sure that rules and regulations are followed throughout the food chain. This helps to protect public health and safety. Here are some examples of different enforcement officers:

1) Factory inspectors — make sure that workplaces stick to health and safety rules. They check the food produced is of a good quality and is presented and labelled properly. They also investigate any accidents or complaints reported.

2) Environmental health officers — visit food factories, shops, restaurants, houses and offices to make sure that they're safe and hygienic. They can withdraw products or close premises if they are a danger to public health. They also monitor pollution levels and help protect the environment.

3) Food technologists — check the content of food that's been produced, e.g. the nutrients or microorganisms it contains. By doing this they can make sure the food is of a good quality and is safe to eat. They also develop new recipes and come up with new ways of making food products.

The Quality and Safety of Food is Very Important

1) If the food is unsafe it could cause food poisoning.
2) If the product isn't the right quality the customers aren't getting what they've paid for.

The Quality of Food is Tested

Enforcement officers check the quality of food at different stages of the food chain (see page 59). In the exam you might need to interpret data from tests used to check the quality of food. For example:

EXAMPLE 1 — storage affects the quality of milk

1) The graph shows the result of an experiment to investigate the freshness of milk that had been stored at different temperatures.
2) The amount of bacteria was measured after 24 hours.
3) The graph shows that the higher the temperature the milk's stored at, the more live bacteria are present in the milk.
4) Line X shows the amount of bacteria that would cause milk to be regarded as unsafe to sell. From the graph you can tell that milk would be unsafe to sell if stored above 8 °C for 24 hours.

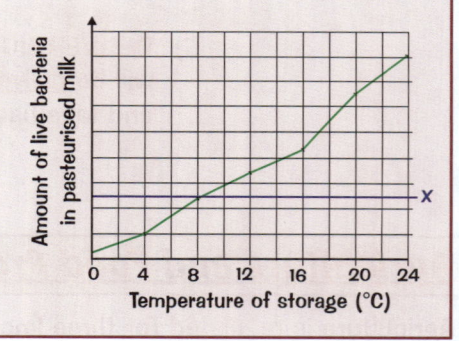

EXAMPLE 2 — storage affects the taste of cheese

1) Taste testing is done to test the quality of cheese.
2) The taste of the cheese is given a score. The higher the score, the better the quality of cheese.
3) A particular type of cheese was tested after it had been stored for different lengths of time.
4) The results show that the quality of the cheese decreases over time.

Number of days in storage	Score for taste
30	6.5
60	6.2
90	5.1

Cheese is an example of a food made by microorganisms (see page 69).

Food's tested at different stages of the food chain, not just during storage.

My biscuits are always safe — I sleep with them under my pillow...

Enforcement officers make sure the food you eat is safe and of a good quality. You need to learn what the three different types of enforcement officers (factory inspectors, environmental health officers, food technologists) do.

Unit 2: Topic 3 — Agriculture and Biotechnology

Organic and Inorganic Farming of Wheat

All farmers want to make money, but some use methods that are more gentle on the environment than others.

Wheat Plants Need the Right Conditions to Grow

1) Farmers are always trying to maximise their crop yields. This means producing as many crops as possible on the land they have available.
2) Lots of farmers in the UK grow wheat. They try to do it in the most efficient way possible, to keep costs down. This means they can sell the wheat on at a competitive price.
3) For wheat to grow at its best, the soil conditions have got to be right:

WATER	NUTRIENTS	pH
Wheat plants need enough water to survive. In the UK it usually rains enough to provide all the water they need. They take up water from the soil through their roots.	Wheat plants need nutrients to help them grow (e.g. nitrates, phosphates and potassium). These are taken up along with water through their roots. Farmers can also add fertilisers to the soil to boost its nutrient content.	The availability of nutrients in the soil is affected by pH. Wheat plants grow best at pH 6-8. If the pH of the soil falls below 6 (i.e. if it becomes more acidic) then the wheat plants won't grow very well at all.

Farmers Can Grow Wheat Using Inorganic or Organic Methods

Inorganic Farming Uses Lots of Artificial Chemicals

Inorganic farming of wheat aims to produce as much wheat as possible from the land and plants available. Lots of artificial chemicals are used, which have risks as well as benefits. For example:

1) **ARTIFICIAL FERTILISERS** — these are chemicals that add nutrients to the soil. Using them means more, healthy wheat plants grow. But the chemicals can be bad for the environment (e.g. they can harm wildlife if they get into rivers and streams).
2) **INSECTICIDES** — these are chemicals that kill insect pests. Insect pests eat the wheat when it's growing. Using insecticides means the crops can grow bigger, but they may also kill other creatures (as well as the insect pests) that aren't eating the wheat.
3) **FUNGICIDES** — these are chemicals that kill fungi which grow on the crops and can cause disease. Fungicides help to keep the crops healthy, which makes them grow bigger.
4) **HERBICIDES** — these are chemicals that kill weeds that grow in the same area as the wheat. If you remove weeds that compete for the same resources (e.g. nutrients from the soil), it means the wheat plants get more resources and so grow better.

Insecticides, fungicides and herbicides are all pesticides. Pesticides are great for helping wheat grow but they can cause unwanted health problems, e.g. for humans who either eat the wheat or eat animals that feed on the wheat.

Organic Farming Doesn't Use Artificial Chemicals

Organic farming of wheat aims to produce as much wheat as possible but in a more traditional way, not using artificial chemicals. For example, organic farming includes:

1) Weeding — weeds are physically removed rather than being sprayed with a herbicide.
2) Using insect-eating creatures, which are put into fields to kill insects that eat crops.
3) Using natural fertilisers, such as manure (animal poo), to add nutrients to the soil.
4) Growing different crops in each field every year — this stops the pests and diseases of one crop building up, and stops nutrients running out (as each crop has slightly different needs).

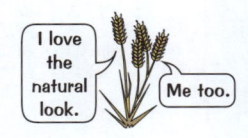

Wheat a minute — you've got to learn this page before you move on...

Make sure you're clear on the two types of farming — inorganic uses artificial chemicals whereas organic doesn't.

Unit 2: Topic 3 — Agriculture and Biotechnology

Wheat Production

Wheat is pretty useful stuff — it's used to make all sorts of everyday foods such as bread and pasta.

Farmers Grow Different Types of Wheat

You need to know about four different types of wheat that are grown to produce food:

1) WINTER WHEAT
- It's planted between September and December and harvested (taken from the field) in the following summer.
- It can withstand cold temperatures.

2) SPRING WHEAT
- It's planted in the spring months and harvested in the summer.
- It can't withstand temperatures as cold as winter wheat.

3) BREAD WHEAT
- It's used to make flour that's used in bread making.
- It contains a lot of a protein called gluten. Gluten gives dough its elasticity (stretchiness) and helps bread to rise.

4) DURUM WHEAT
- It's used to produce flour that's used to make pasta.
- It doesn't contain a lot of gluten.

There are Several Stages to Wheat Production

Whatever type of wheat's being produced, there are five main stages needed to produce it:

1) Soil preparation — the soil has to be ploughed to prepare it.

2) Sowing (planting the wheat seeds).

3) Using chemicals — fertilisers and pesticides (see page 61) can be added to the field so that as much wheat as possible is produced.

4) Harvesting — the wheat is cut down and collected.

5) Drying and storing — the grain is dried and stored in buildings until it's ready to be used (e.g. to make flour).

What do you say when you drop a piece of bread?...Oh crumbs...

Next time you're in the supermarket have a look at all the different sorts of flour you can get. There are loads. Different types of flour are used to produce different types of food like bread, pasta and cakes. Yum yum.

Unit 2: Topic 3 — Agriculture and Biotechnology

More on Wheat Production

Wheat farmers need to be pretty nifty with a calculator as well as a tractor.

Germination Rates Help a Farmer Decide How Many Seeds to Sow

1) Not all seeds that are sown will start to grow (germinate).
2) The percentage of seeds sown that are likely to germinate can be calculated — this is called the germination rate. Different varieties of wheat have different germination rates.
3) Knowing the germination rate helps the farmer to work out how many seeds they need to sow to grow a certain number of wheat plants. It can also help them to choose between different varieties of wheat seed.

EXAMPLE

Farmer Frett planted 80 seeds of wheat A. 60 of them germinated.
She used this information to work out the germination rate of wheat A:

$$\text{germination rate} = \frac{\text{number of seeds that germinated}}{\text{number of seeds planted}} \times 100 = \frac{60}{80} \times 100 = 75\%$$

She then compared this germination rate to another two types of wheat.
She decided to sow seeds from wheat B because it has the highest germination rate.

Wheat	Germination rate (%)
A	75
B	82
C	67

Farmers Can Work Out Yield by Weighing their Wheat

1) A farmer can work out how much wheat they produce in total from their land (their wheat yield).
2) They do this by calculating the dry mass of the wheat. This is the mass of the wheat once all the water has been removed.
3) It would be hard work to dry out and weigh all the wheat plants on their land. Instead they just work out the dry mass of the wheat plants in a small sample area, then get busy with their calculator:

EXAMPLE

Farmer Frew weighs out 1 kg of wheat taken from his field. He dries the wheat out and weighs it again. Now its mass is 800 g (this is its dry mass). Next he works out the percentage dry mass of his wheat:

$$\text{percentage dry mass} = \frac{\text{dry mass}}{\text{original mass}} \times 100 = \frac{800 \text{ g}}{1000 \text{ g}} \times 100 = 80\%$$

Remember 1 kg = 1000 g

He has 10 hectares of land. He knows that one hectare of his land produces 4 tonnes of wheat. So now he knows the percentage dry mass of his wheat, he can work out the total dry mass of wheat he can produce on his land:

Total mass of wheat on his land = 10 × 4 = 40 tonnes.

80% of 40 tonnes = $\frac{80}{100} \times 40$ = 32 tonnes.

He can use this information to compare wheat yields for different years.

Year	Wheat Yield (tonnes of dry mass)
2010	36
2011	41
2012	32

Farmers Have to Work Out How Much of a Chemical They Need

1) The chemicals that farmers use on their wheat (e.g. fertilisers, pesticides) need to be diluted (mixed with water) before they can be used.
2) Farmers have to work out how much of each undiluted chemical they need to buy.

EXAMPLE

A farmer has 50 hectares of land.
He needs 40 litres of diluted fertiliser per hectare.
So he needs 50 × 40 = 2000 litres of diluted fertiliser.
To dilute this particular fertiliser, he needs 1 part fertiliser for every 1000 parts water.
So he needs to buy: $\frac{2000}{1000}$ = 2 litres of the undiluted fertiliser to cover his land.

Unit 2: Topic 3 — Agriculture and Biotechnology

Rearing Cattle For Milk

Dairy farmers keep cows so they can sell the milk they produce. The way they look after the cows and the type of cows they keep affect the milk that's produced.

Four Factors Affect Animal Growth

Cows are bred to produce large quantities of milk. Farmers can increase animal growth and milk yield if they understand what animals need to grow:

1) Warmth — animals grow faster if they don't waste energy keeping warm.
2) Shelter — animals grow faster if they have shelter to keep them warm.
3) Food and water — both food and water are needed to provide energy to grow.
4) Good health — pests and diseases can weaken animals, slowing down growth or killing them.

In the exam you might be asked to interpret data about product yield from cattle (e.g. how much milk cows produce).

E.g. Farmer Giles tested three different types of feed to see which would give the greatest product yield in his cows. Three types of feed were fed to three groups of cows and the average increase in yearly milk production per cow was calculated for each group. Using the table you can see that to get the greatest product yield (most milk) from his cows Farmer Giles should use feed C.

Type of Feed	Average increase in yearly milk production per cow (litres)
A	670
B	705
C	800

Some Cows Are Better Than Others At Producing Milk

1) Farmers want their cows to be able to produce lots of good quality milk.
2) They also want to spend as little money as possible on keeping the cows.
3) Different breeds of cows have different characteristics (features).
4) Characteristics can affect how much milk the cows can produce and the quality of the milk.
5) Choosing breeds of cows with good characteristics will improve productivity because they'll produce the highest yield of good quality milk for the least amount of money.

Cows kept for producing milk usually have some of the following characteristics...

1) Able to produce lots of milk.
2) Can live for a long time — so they can produce milk for a good number of years.
3) Are in good health and don't get many diseases.
4) Able to produce good quality milk with cheaper sources of food (e.g. by grazing on poorer pasture land).
5) Are quite small — small cows need less space (so they cost the farmer less to keep).

What do you get if you shake a cow?...Milkshake...Hilarious, I know...

Farmers might seem pretty picky about the cattle they keep but they don't keep them for fun — they're trying to make money. If you moooove on to the next page you'll find out how farmers 'create' the best breeds.

Unit 2: Topic 3 — Agriculture and Biotechnology

Breeding Cattle

Farmers choose which cows and bulls to mate together so they end up with a breed that's best at producing milk. It's not a very romantic way of breeding but it means we get lots of good quality milk at low prices.

Selective Breeding is Used By Dairy Farmers to Increase Productivity

Selective breeding is when humans select the plants or animals that are going to breed and flourish, according to what we want from them. Dairy farmers selectively breed their cattle so they get cows that produce lots of good quality milk. Here's the basic process involved in selective breeding:

1) From the existing stock, the organisms that have the best characteristics are selected (see previous page).
2) They're bred with each other.
3) The best of the offspring are selected and bred.
4) This process is repeated over several generations to develop the desired traits.

Cattle Can be Bred Using Artificial Insemination

Artificial insemination (AI) of cattle means cows can get pregnant without actually having to, erm... you know, have sexy time. Artificial insemination involves four stages:

1) **Selection of animals** — animals with the best characteristics (see p.64).
2) **Collection of sperm** — the sperm is collected into a device that stimulates the bull to ejaculate and then keeps the sperm at the right temperature.
3) **Storage of sperm** — the sperm is checked for quality, to make sure it will fertilise the cow. It's then placed in disposable plastic straws, which are frozen in liquid nitrogen (-196 °C) until the sperm are required.
4) **Insertion of sperm** — to inseminate the cow a long pipette is used to insert the contents of the straw. The cow must be inseminated at the right time, just before she is about to release an egg, to increase the chances of fertilisation happening.

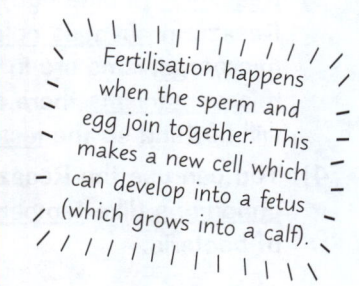

Fertilisation happens when the sperm and egg join together. This makes a new cell which can develop into a fetus (which grows into a calf).

Artificial Insemination has Advantages over Natural Mating

Advantages of artificial insemination include:

1) **Reduced cost** — it's cheaper and safer for the farmer to buy semen than keep a male animal.
2) **Decreased risk of disease** — the risk of exposure to sexually-transmitted diseases is reduced.
3) **Increased quality** — the sperm is of known quality from a tested, high quality bull.

Selective breeding — sounds like a night out at my local disco...

Selective breeding and artificial insemination are useful methods for the farmers (and for you, if you're a milk drinker). Learn the steps involved in selective breeding and artificial insemination, and make sure you know how these methods help the farmers to produce cattle with desired traits (like being able to produce lots of milk).

Unit 2: Topic 3 — Agriculture and Biotechnology

Processing Milk

Even fresh milk that you buy in shops isn't actually straight-from-the-cow fresh — it goes through several stages to make sure it's safe before you pour it on your cornflakes.

Milk is Processed Before It's Sold In Shops

Milk can contain harmful bacteria, which could make you really ill if you drank it. Also milk can contain quite a lot of fat, which can be bad for your health if you drink a lot of it. Luckily there are several processes that milk can go through before it's sold to help keep everyone healthy.

PASTEURISATION

Pasteurisation involves heating milk up to about 70 °C for about 20 seconds, and then cooling it. This kills off most harmful bacteria, so the product shouldn't make you ill, and it also makes the milk last longer before it goes off.

ULTRA HIGH TEMPERATURE (UHT) PROCESSING

UHT processing involves heating milk up to very high temperatures of about 135 °C for about one second. This kills off all the harmful bacteria and makes the milk last longer (even longer than pasteurised milk).

REMOVING FAT

Much of the fat in milk rises to the surface as cream. Some of this layer of cream can be skimmed off (removed) so the milk that's left contains less fat. By removing different amounts of cream, different types of milk are produced, e.g. semi-skimmed milk (1.7% fat) and skimmed milk (about 0.2% fat).

You Can Test the Freshness of Milk

1) Drinking milk that isn't fresh can make you ill because it tends to contain a lot of microorganisms (e.g. bacteria).
2) The Resazurin test is used to test the freshness of milk.
3) Resazurin (a blue dye) is added to a sample of milk. Resazurin changes colour depending on how many microorganisms are in the milk sample — the more microorganisms there are, the greater the colour change will be (and so the less fresh the milk will be).
4) You can use the Resazurin test to look at how different conditions (like temperature or pH) affect the growth of bacteria.

Colour of dye	
Blue	Least microorganisms (fresh)
Lilac	
Mauve	
Pink	
Colourless	Most microorganisms (not fresh)

EXAMPLE: Investigating how temperature affects bacterial growth in milk.

1) Pour 10 cm³ of fresh milk into three test tubes labelled A, B and C. Add 1 cm³ of resazurin dye to each tube and mix well.
2) Store tube A at a temperature of 3 °C, tube B at 10 °C and tube C at 25 °C.
3) Record the colour of the dye in the tubes at set intervals, e.g. after 0, 24, 48 and 72 hours.

Use sterile test tubes and the same batch of milk to keep the test fair.

Results:

Time (hours)	0	24	48	72
Tube A	Blue	Blue	Blue	Lilac
Tube B	Blue	Lilac	Mauve	Pink
Tube C	Blue	Mauve	Pink	Colourless

Tube A changed colour the least — so the growth of bacteria is slowest at 3 °C.
Tube C changed colour the most — so the growth of bacteria is fastest at 25 °C.

This suggests that storing milk in a fridge, instead of at room temperature, will slow the growth of bacteria — keeping it fresher for longer.

Make sure that you've learnt this page by running it past your eyes*...

So milk gets processed quite a bit before you drink it. And it's a good job it does — it could make you really poorly if there were loads of bacteria or other microorganisms growing in it. And you wouldn't want that.

Unit 2: Topic 3 — Agriculture and Biotechnology

*'Past your eyes' sounds like 'pasteurise'. It's funny.

Microorganisms — Uses and Dangers

Believe it or not, microorganisms can be very useful. But if they're not controlled properly, they can cause lots of problems (much like a two year old child).

Microorganisms Can Help Us Make Lots of Useful Products...

Microorganisms include bacteria, fungi (including yeasts) and viruses.
We can make useful products from (or with the help of) microorganisms. For example:

1) Food — e.g. bread, cheese, yoghurt and mycoprotein.
2) Alcohol — for drink, e.g. beer and wine, or fuel, e.g. ethanol (which is mixed with petrol to make gasohol).
3) Enzymes — e.g. chymosin, used in cheese making.

...But They Can Also Cause Disease and Food Spoilage

1) Some microorganisms cause diseases, e.g. the flu virus causes flu.
2) Some bacteria and fungi can cause food to "go off" — this is called food spoilage.
3) Food can be spoilt by visible growth, e.g. mould on bread.
4) Food spoilage is also caused by waste products. Microorganisms can break down the food and feed on it, producing waste products that contaminate the food.
5) Some microorganisms can make you ill if you ingest them — causing food poisoning.
6) In the exam you might be asked to interpret data about outbreaks of food poisoning:

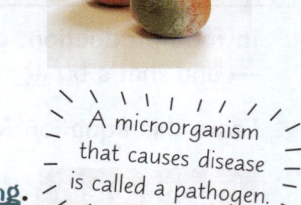

A microorganism that causes disease is called a pathogen.

EXAMPLE

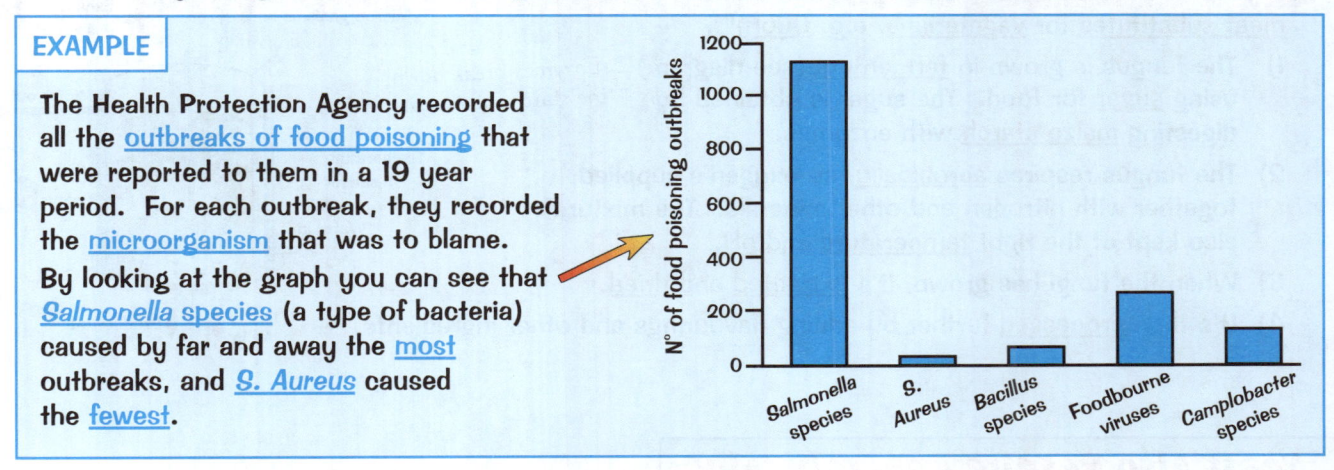

The Health Protection Agency recorded all the outbreaks of food poisoning that were reported to them in a 19 year period. For each outbreak, they recorded the microorganism that was to blame.
By looking at the graph you can see that Salmonella species (a type of bacteria) caused by far and away the most outbreaks, and S. Aureus caused the fewest.

Contamination Has to be Avoided in Food Production

When you're growing specific microorganisms for food production you don't want other types sneaking in and messing things up.

1) Contamination in food production could allow dangerous microorganisms to grow in the food.
2) Aseptic techniques are used to make sure things are kept clean and sterile.
3) There are several ways you can make things sterile, e.g. using heat or chemicals, which kills the microorganisms. It's important to sterilise all equipment before and after use, and mixtures can be boiled — this is done before the useful microorganism is added, or else it'd be killed as well.

Hitting your food with a hammer — another way to cause food spoilage...

Microorganisms can help to make lots of everyday foods (mmm, cheeeese). But it's very important that unwanted microorganisms don't get into your food (otherwise you might get food poisoning and believe me, that ain't nice). Thankfully aseptic techniques are used in food production to keep you as disease-free as possible.

Unit 2: Topic 3 — Agriculture and Biotechnology

Products From Microorganisms

Microorganisms can help us make some really tasty food products — and it's another ideal topic for examiners to give you some info to interpret. There are loads of examples on these two pages...

Microorganisms Need the Right Conditions to Make Food Products

1) Microorganisms convert sugar into other substances during respiration (a process that releases energy). There are two types — aerobic (with oxygen) and anaerobic (without oxygen).
2) In industry, this process is called fermentation and it's done in a machine called a fermenter (see below).
3) Some products are made from the microorganisms themselves, e.g. mycoprotein (see below). Others are a product that they make, e.g. yeast extract (see below).
4) Microorganisms need the right conditions for fermentation, i.e. a food source, the right temperature, and oxygen if it's respiring aerobically.

The big, fancy fermenters used in industry can also be called bioreactors (see page 71).

Yeast Grow Quickest When Respiring Aerobically

In food production, you want the microorganisms to grow as fast as possible — and that's by aerobic respiration.

Learn this equation for aerobic respiration: ⟶ | sugar + oxygen → carbon dioxide + water |

Mycoprotein

Mycoprotein is a product from fungi that's used to make meat substitutes for vegetarians, e.g. Quorn™.

1) The fungus is grown in fermenters (see diagram) using sugar for food. The sugar is obtained by digesting maize starch with enzymes.
2) The fungus respires aerobically, so oxygen's supplied, together with nitrogen and other minerals. The mixture's also kept at the right temperature and pH.
3) When the fungi has grown, it's extracted and dried.
4) It's then processed further by adding flavourings and other ingredients.

Enzymes break down the starch into sugars.

(Diagram labels: Food in, Microorganisms in, Exhaust gases out, Water out, Temperature sensor, pH probe, Water in, Air in, Product out)

Yeast Also Respire Anaerobically

Anaerobic fermentation by yeast helps us make yeast extract — a product that's used to improve the flavour of many foods.

Learn the equation for anaerobic respiration in yeast: ⟶ | sugar → ethanol + carbon dioxide |

Yeast extract

1) Sugar is added to a sample of yeast and it's left to ferment — this process makes alcoholic drinks such as beer.
2) After fermentation, the remaining yeast cells are processed by having their cell walls removed. The product that's left is called yeast extract.

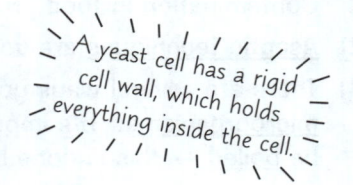

A yeast cell has a rigid cell wall, which holds everything inside the cell.

Yeast-aday, all my troubles seemed so far away...

So microorganisms such as yeast can respire with or without oxygen. There are two important word equations (the things in white boxes with → and + signs in) to learn on this page — so you'd better get learning them...

Unit 2: Topic 3 — Agriculture and Biotechnology

More Products From Microorganisms

Fermentation doesn't only occur in yeast. Bacteria do it too — only their anaerobic fermentation is slightly different. However it's done, the chemicals produced in fermentation are pretty handy for making food.

Anaerobic Fermentation in Bacteria Produces Acid

Anaerobic fermentation in some bacteria (e.g. *Lactobaccili*) help us make cheese and yoghurt. Anaerobic respiration in these bacteria produces lactic acid.

Here's the equation to learn: ➡ sugar → lactic acid

Cheese

You need to know the steps involved in cheese making, so here goes...
1) A culture of bacteria is added to warm milk.
2) They turn the sugar in the milk into lactic acid, which causes the milk to curdle.
3) Enzymes (e.g. chymosin) are often added to help produce solid curds in the milk.
4) These curds are separated from the liquid whey.
5) The curd is left to ripen for a while before it's processed.

Yoghurt

Yoghurt is basically fermented milk. Here's how it's made:
1) Milk is pasteurised (heated) to kill any unwanted microorganisms (see p.66). All the equipment is also sterilised (see p.67). Then the milk's cooled.
2) A culture of bacteria is added and the mixture is incubated (heated to about 40 °C) in a fermenter.
3) The bacteria turn the sugar in the milk into lactic acid, causing the milk to clot and solidify into yoghurt.
4) Flavours (e.g. fruit) and colours are sometimes added before the yoghurt is packaged.

Enzymes Produced in Fermentation Help With Food Production

When they ferment, some microorganisms also produce enzymes which are pretty handy in food production.

Coffee

1) Coffee is produced from coffee beans which grow on plants (coffee plants, surprisingly enough).
2) The coffee beans have a slimy layer called mucilage stuck to them.
3) To remove the mucilage, the coffee beans are left to ferment.
4) In this process, microorganisms present on the beans respire and produce enzymes. The enzymes break down the mucilage so it goes all mushy.
5) The mucilage is then washed away and the beans are dried and processed to produce the coffee we know and love.

Soya sauce

1) Soya sauce is a dark liquid used in cooking. It's made from soya beans using microorganisms.
2) Soya beans have cultures of microorganisms added to them. The microorganisms ferment and produce enzymes. Over time, these enzymes break down substances in the beans (e.g. proteins) so the beans go soft.
3) The mushy soya beans are then processed and the liquid is drained off to produce soya sauce.

The world's fastest yoghurt — pasteurised before you see it...

By now you should be convinced that microorganisms are really quite useful when it comes to food production. But you still need to stop some microorganisms infecting your food — that's why milk is pasteurised.

Unit 2: Topic 3 — Agriculture and Biotechnology

Growth of Microorganisms

To use microorganisms (e.g. bacteria), food producers have to be good at growing them (lots and lots of them).

Bacteria Reproduce Really, Really Fast

Bacteria reproduce by splitting in two, so the number of bacteria doubles at regular intervals. This means their growth is exponential — to start with, there's only a handful of bacteria but soon there are millions of them. In the exam you might have to do some calculations on this kind of thing. E.g:

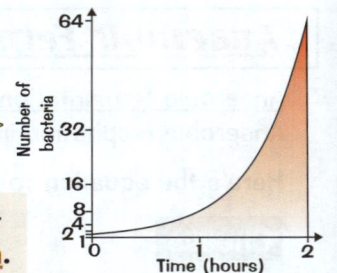

In certain conditions, one bacterium reproduces itself every 20 minutes. A scientist wants to know how many bacteria he will have in 1 hour if he starts with 30 bacteria.
So in 20 minutes he will have 30 × 2 = 60 bacteria.
In 40 minutes he will have 60 × 2 = 120 bacteria.
And in 1 hour (60 minutes) he will have 120 × 2 = 240 bacteria.

The Growth of a Population of Microorganisms Happens in Stages

To be able to make food products from microorganisms, there needs to be a lot of them. When a population of one type of microorganism is grown under controlled conditions the microorganisms are called a culture. The growth of a culture of microorganisms happens in several stages:

① Lag phase — growth is very slow as the speed at which the microorganisms are reproducing (the reproduction rate) is slow. The microorganisms are adjusting to the new conditions.

② Exponential growth phase — growth is very fast as microorganisms are reproducing very quickly. The conditions for growth are at their best during this phase.

③ Stationary phase — growth levels off as the reproduction rate is the same as the death rate. There are loads of microorganisms now, and there are not enough nutrients to keep them all alive and reproducing.

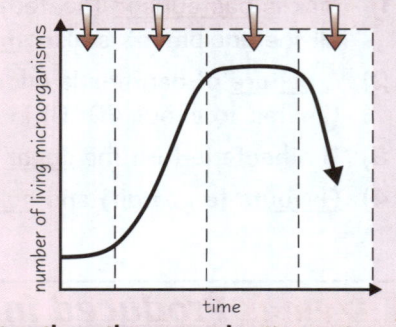

④ Senescence (death phase) — growth falls as the death rate is faster than the reproduction rate. While they're growing microorganisms produce harmful products. By this stage these products have built up and cause lots of microorganisms to die. Also, by this stage lots of the nutrients that were available have been used up — this causes more microorganisms to die.

There Are Different Ways of Growing Microorganisms

You need to know about two different ways of growing microorganisms:

① BATCH CULTURE — nutrients are added at the start of the process and the culture is grown until it reaches the stationary phase. All the microorganisms (the batch) are then taken out, the equipment is cleaned and sterilised and then a new batch is grown.

② CONTINUOUS CULTURE — the culture is continuously grown. Nutrients are continuously added to the culture and the product is continuously removed. This keeps the culture in the exponential stage of growth (so it never reaches the stationary phase).

Which method is used depends on the microorganism being grown and what is wanted from them, e.g. some microorganisms only produce useful products during the stationary phase. There are advantages and disadvantages of each method. For example:

	BATCH CULTURE	CONTINUOUS CULTURE
Advantage	Easy to set up and run.	Get lots of product.
Disadvantage	No product is made whilst the equipment is being cleaned out.	Expensive to set up and run.

Unit 2: Topic 3 — Agriculture and Biotechnology

Bioreactor Conditions

When microorganisms are grown by the food industry, it's best if they grow as fast as possible. For this to happen, the conditions where the microorganisms live have to be just right.

Bioreactors Are Used to Grow Microorganisms

1) Microorganisms need the right conditions to grow at their fastest (e.g. the right pH and temperature).
2) When they're grown in industry, big machines called bioreactors (fermenters) are used for fermentation.
3) Using a bioreactor means the conditions that microorganisms live in can be monitored and controlled.

Bioreactors Have Sensors to Monitor Conditions

1) Conditions inside a bioreactor are monitored with sensors.
2) These pick up information about the conditions inside the bioreactor such as the pH and temperature.
3) They pass the information to a computer and data logging software displays the information.
4) The computer knows what level the pH and temperature inside the bioreactor should be.
5) If the pH or temperature is not at the right level, the computer triggers a response which causes the conditions to be returned to the right level. The computer may also trigger an alarm so that people working with the bioreactor know something's wrong with the conditions inside it.
6) This process can be shown in a flow diagram like this one:

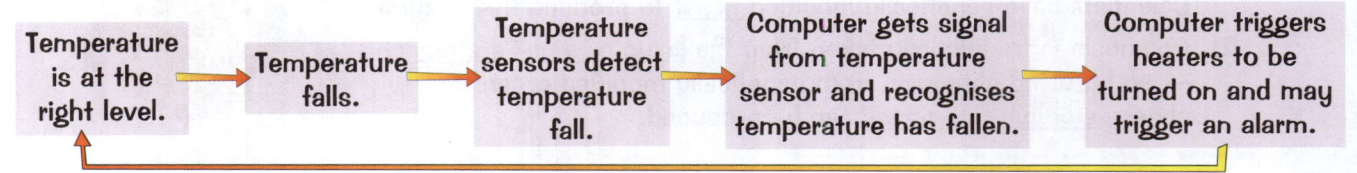

Temperature is at the right level. → Temperature falls. → Temperature sensors detect temperature fall. → Computer gets signal from temperature sensor and recognises temperature has fallen. → Computer triggers heaters to be turned on and may trigger an alarm.

Temperature rises.

A Bioreactor's Computer Produces Graphs

Information about the conditions inside the bioreactor can be displayed on a graph. In the exam you might be asked to interpret data about a graph produced by a bioreactor's computer. For example:

1) The graph shows the pH readings from inside a bioreactor over one day.
2) When the sensors detect that the pH has fallen too far below the right level, the computer sends signals to the bioreactor to increase the pH.
3) The points on the graph marked with a red cross show the times this happened.

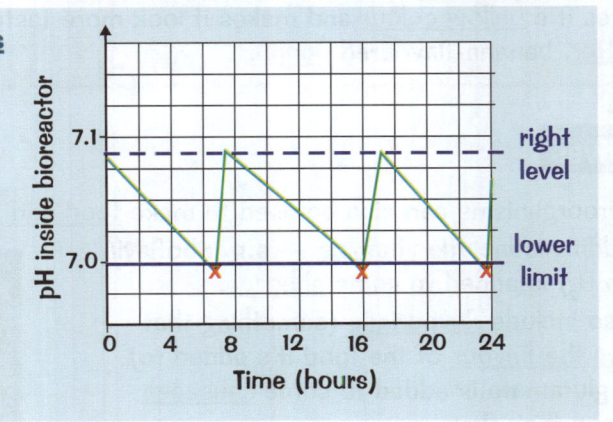

Bed, check, crisps, check, TV, check — just monitoring my conditions...

Imagine a world where we all lived in bioreactors — whenever you were too hot or needed more food or more music the bioreactor would just sort it out for you. But unfortunately, you don't have a life as cushy as a microorganism — you have to do things for yourself (like learning this page... inside out and back to front).

Unit 2: Topic 3 — Agriculture and Biotechnology

Genetically Modified Microorganisms

Microorganisms can be altered to make them even more useful in food production.

Genetically Modified Organisms Make Useful Proteins...

We can produce large amounts of useful proteins (e.g. chymosin) from microorganisms by modifying their DNA (their genetic material).

1) Each gene (a short section of DNA) codes for a particular protein in an organism.
2) A gene for a useful protein is selected and added into the genetic material of a microorganism.
3) The genetically modified (GM) microorganism can then produce this protein.

...Which Can Be Used in Food Production

1) The food industry grows GM microorganisms on a large scale.
2) This produces lots of the useful protein, which can then be used in food production.
3) Here are some examples of some useful things that GM microorganisms are used to produce:

Enzymes

1) The enzyme chymosin is used in cheese making — it clots the milk. Scientists have genetically modified yeast to produce this enzyme.
2) Chymosin is traditionally taken from the lining of a calf's stomach — so by using chymosin from genetically modified organisms, cheese suitable for vegans can be produced.

Food colourings

1) Beta-carotene is a yellow pigment (colour) found in plants.
2) The gene for beta-carotene can be taken from plants and inserted into a microorganism's DNA.
3) Lots of the microorganisms can be grown and then, hey presto, there's lots of beta-carotene ready to be added to your food.
4) This gives it a yellow colour and makes it look more tasty, e.g. butter, banana-flavoured yoghurt.

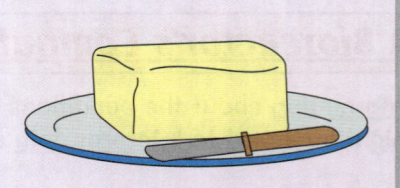

Food additives

1) GM microorganisms can also be used to make food additives.
2) Food additives include vitamins — e.g. riboflavin (vitamin B$_2$) is added to some cheeses.
3) They also include flavourings (something that improves the flavour of the food it's added to) — e.g. glutamate is added to some sausages to improve their flavour.

GCSE teachers like microorganisms — they make useful pro-teens...

Wow, these microorganisms really are amazing. Their genes are altered so they can make loads of the things that are added to our foods. They make foods look nicer and taste better — three cheers for microorganisms, I say.

Unit 2: Topic 3 — Agriculture and Biotechnology

Revision Summary

Hmm... so this whole farming lark, what's that all about? Well, if you don't know, you haven't read this section properly, and your first task is to go back and read it all again. While you're at it, check you know your biotechnology stuff as well. When you think you know your stuff, here are some delightful questions for you...

1) a) Name two crops that are grown by British farmers.
   b) For each crop, give an example of a food product that it's used to produce.
2) Suggest two uses of biotechnology to produce food.
3) What are the five stages in the chain of food production?
4) Give three reasons why agriculture is regulated.
5) Why is it important that enforcement officers monitor the food chain?
6) Describe what an environmental health officer does.
7) Give two reasons why it's important that the quality and safety of food is checked.
8) What three soil conditions have to be right for wheat to grow at its best?
9) How is organic farming different from inorganic farming?
10) Explain why farmers use insecticides.
11) List four different types of wheat.
12) Briefly describe the five stages of wheat production.
13) *A farmer plants 600 wheat seeds that have a germination rate of 85%.
    Work out how many wheat seeds the farmer will expect to germinate.
14) What is meant by the 'dry mass' of wheat?
15) What four factors affect animal growth?
16) List two characteristics a farmer may look for in dairy cows that he wants to selectively breed.
17) Describe the basic process of selective breeding.
18) Describe the four stages involved in artificial insemination.
19) Suggest one benefit of artificial insemination compared to natural mating.
20) Explain how milk is pasteurised.
21) What can the Resazurin test be used for?
22) Name two useful products from microorganisms.
23) Why are aseptic techniques used when growing specific microorganisms?
24) Write down the word equation for:
    a) aerobic respiration in yeast.
    b) anaerobic respiration in yeast.
25) What is mycoprotein?
26) Write down the word equation for anaerobic respiration in bacteria.
27) Explain how fermentation is involved in the production of:
    a) cheese,
    b) coffee.
28) Outline the four stages of growth in a culture of microorganisms.
29) Give one advantage and one disadvantage of continuous cultures.
30) Give two conditions that bioreactors monitor and control.
31) Describe how microorganisms can be modified to produce useful proteins.
32) Give two example of useful food products that can be made by genetically modified microorganisms.

* Answers on p.108.

Unit 2: Topic 3 — Agriculture and Biotechnology

% Unit 2: Topic 4 — Making Chemical Products

The Chemical Industry

At last, a section all about smellies — bubble bath, soaps and bath salts. Lovely. Well... and fertilisers, drugs and toilet cleaners — basically any kind of product that has been made at a chemical plant. Not so lovely...

Different People Help to Make a Chemical Product

A chemical plant is an industrial site where one or more chemical products are made. Here, the product is made on an industrial (large) scale using special equipment. People needed to make the product include:

1) Research chemists — they do the research (figure out what to make and how to make it) for new chemical products, e.g. new types of shampoo.
2) Chemical engineers — they design the manufacturing processes needed to make the chemical product on an industrial scale and make sure the processes are safe, efficient and actually make money.

In a chemical plant, laboratory (lab) technicians help research chemists and chemical engineers to do their jobs. A lab technician's role is varied and includes:

Lab technicians work in other labs too, e.g. ones in schools.

- Making product formulations — they mix the ingredients of a product together following a fixed formula.
- Sampling — they take samples of a new product, or a product that is being made by a new method, for testing and analysis (see below).
- Testing and analysis — they test the samples and analyse the results. E.g. they may test a sample from a new product formulation to make sure it has the right qualities.
- Using and maintaining equipment — they know how to use a variety of lab equipment and are responsible for keeping it safe to use and in working order.
- Storing and handling chemicals safely — chemicals used to make a product can be dangerous. Lab technicians know which chemicals are dangerous, and how to handle and store them safely. E.g. some chemicals can only be used in a fume cupboard, other chemicals need to be stored in a fridge.

There are Lots of Other Jobs in the Chemical Industry

A chemical plant is a business. People with a wide range of skills and qualifications are needed to get the chemical product made and then out to the consumer (the person who buys it). For example:

1) The plant manager — he or she oversees the daily running of a chemical plant.
2) Marketing and sales people — they market (advertise) and sell the chemical products to other companies and the public.
3) Finance officers — they manage the chemical plant's finances (money).
4) Healthy and safety officers — they are responsible for the health and safety of staff at the plant, e.g. they make sure health and safety regulations are followed.

The Location of a Chemical Plant is Important

Chances are there might be a chemical plant close to where you live. They don't pop up just anywhere though because they need to have certain things close by, such as:

- raw materials
- skilled workers
- good transport links (e.g. road, rail)
- landfill sites (for waste disposal)
- water (to cool down the process)
- a source of power (e.g. electricity)

A chemical plant can be good for the local community because, e.g. it may provide new jobs, new transport links, and cause new homes and businesses to be built. Chemical plants also bring in lots of money to the UK economy.

It's really handy that they make deodorant up the road...

The chemical industry is a pretty complex thing. It's all well and good to have all the bits of equipment that are needed, but you wouldn't get very far without also having all the different people in their jobs. Many scientists, researchers, managers and officers are there to make the whole process work smoothly.

Regulating the Chemical Industry

Some chemicals are harmful to people, animals or plants — and so care must be taken when working with them. People who work with chemicals have to be aware of lots of rules about how to handle them.

Governments Regulate the Manufacture and Use of Chemicals

To protect us and the world around us, governments create laws and guidelines for people working with chemicals. These are designed to:

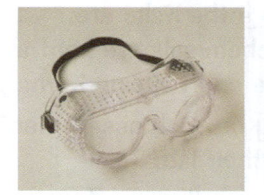

1) Limit our exposure to dangerous chemicals.
2) Prevent dangerous chemicals from getting into the environment.
3) Reduce the chance of accidents happening.
4) Minimise the damage caused if an accident does happen.

The Health and Safety Executive Regulates Chemical Industries

The Health and Safety Executive (HSE) is an organisation set up by the UK government to protect people's health at their school or workplace. One of its jobs is to make sure that when people work with chemicals, they protect themselves and the public from any danger. The HSE checks that safety rules are being followed by any company that works with chemicals. For example:

1) Companies producing agrochemicals (fertilisers and pesticides for farms).
2) Pharmaceutical companies producing medicines.
3) Oil refineries making petrol, diesel and other chemicals from crude oil. 
4) Companies producing household chemicals such as cleaning products.
5) Laboratories in schools, colleges and universities.

Laws Require People to Work Safely with Chemicals

Inspectors from the HSE visit places where chemicals are used. They check that chemicals are being handled and stored properly. During a visit an inspector may do several things.

1) If there are any minor safety problems, an inspector can give advice on how to work even more safely.

2) If an accident has been reported, an inspector can carry out an investigation to find out what caused the accident and what needs to be done to stop the same accident happening again in the future.

3) If there are serious safety problems, or laws about how to use or store certain chemicals are being broken, an inspector can force the company to stop working straight away. They will only be allowed to start work again when the inspector has seen that all of the safety problems have been solved.

Skiving chemistry — reducing the danger of chemicals...

...but it's not advisable though. You'll just be increasing the danger of not doing too great in your exam. Now, on to the important stuff — you won't be expected to remember any particular rules and regulations — just be aware that they exist and understand why it's important to follow them carefully. It's all about being safe.

Unit 2: Topic 4 — Making Chemical Products

Risk Assessments and Hazchem Symbols

People who work with chemicals have to follow health and safety regulations (see previous page). These regulations say that risk assessments must be carried out...

A Risk Assessment Identifies Hazards and Reduces Risks

1) A hazard is something that could cause harm (e.g. a highly flammable chemical).
2) A risk is the harm that could be caused (e.g. burns).
3) A risk assessment involves identifying hazards, assessing how likely and how severe the risks are, and suggesting ways of avoiding or reducing those risks. (E.g. highly flammable chemicals are kept away from flames and stored in flameproof, metal containers to avoid them catching fire and causing burns.)
4) The health and safety officer (see p.74) in a chemical plant makes sure staff carry out risk assessments for their area of work, e.g. a lab technician might carry out a risk assessment for their lab.
5) The staff then follow the 'how to reduce/avoid the risk' part of the risk assessment as they work, to avoid any accidents.
6) Dangerous chemicals are labelled with hazchem symbols (see below). Information about how to use, store and transport these chemicals safely is given on the risk assessment.

You Need to Learn the Common Hazchem Symbols

Lots of chemicals can be bad for you or dangerous in some way. These hazchem symbols might just save your skin...

Oxidising
Provides oxygen which allows other materials to burn more fiercely.
Example: Liquid oxygen.

Highly Flammable
Catches fire easily.
Example: Petrol.

Toxic
Can cause death either by swallowing, breathing in, or absorption through the skin.
Example: Hydrogen cyanide.

Explosive
Will explode.
Example: Fireworks, TNT, parents, etc.

Harmful
Like toxic but not quite as dangerous.
Example: Copper sulfate.

Corrosive
Attacks and destroys living tissues, including eyes and skin.
Example: Concentrated sulfuric acid.

Irritant
Not corrosive but can cause reddening or blistering of the skin.
Examples: Bleach, children, etc.

Hazchem symbols are shown on tankers used to transport chemicals to and from chemical plants. This means that if there's an accident causing a chemical spillage, the emergency services will know what type of chemical has spilled so they can clear it up safely. Next to the hazchem symbol will be other information such as:

An emergency action code — this code tells the emergency services how to deal with the spillage.

A UN substance identification number — this identifies the chemical in the tanker.

```
3YE
1270
0128 077512
```

A specialist advice line — this is a telephone number that the emergency services can ring to get more advice on the dangers posed by the chemical and the clean up.

Toxic — the right symbol for revision...

Hazchem symbols are clear and simple, and the same symbols are used internationally (all over the world). So if I was in a different country and saw an explosive symbol on a tub, I wouldn't strike a match next to it...

Unit 2: Topic 4 — Making Chemical Products

Industrial Production of Chemicals

We use loads of important chemicals like fertilisers every year — and they don't just fall off the back of a wagon (unless you're following a horse box). No, they have to be extracted or made...

Metals are Extracted from Ores

1) Rocks are made of minerals. Minerals are just solid elements and compounds.
2) Metal ores are rocks that contain minerals that metals can be extracted from.
3) Copper is extracted from copper ore. Copper is used to make things like pipes and electrical wiring.
4) Iron is extracted from iron ore. Iron is used a lot in the building industry, e.g. to make bridges. It can also be used to make steel, which is used to make loads of things, e.g. cars.
5) Copper and iron can be used to make insoluble salts (see pages 82-83) and soluble salts (see page 84).

Some Chemicals are Produced on a Large Scale...

There are certain chemicals that we produce thousands and thousands of tonnes of every year. Chemicals that are produced on a large scale are called bulk chemicals — ammonia, sulfuric acid and sodium hydroxide are three examples.

> The chemical industry needs to make a fair bit of ammonia to meet the demand. It is used in many industrial processes, including the production of nitric acid and fertiliser.

> You may have come across sulfuric acid in the lab at school. You might not think it, but sulfuric acid also has to be produced on a very large scale. As well as being a lab chemical, it has many other uses including the production of fertiliser, detergents and some medicines.

> Another chemical produced on a very large scale is sodium hydroxide — again you may have come across this in the lab, but it's also used to make things like soap and ceramics.

Ammonia, sulfuric acid and sodium hydroxide are inorganic chemicals — like most inorganic chemicals, they don't contain carbon. Other chemicals are organic — they do contain carbon, e.g. crude oil.

...And Some are Produced on a Smaller Scale

Some chemicals aren't needed in such large amounts — but that doesn't mean they're any less important.

1) Chemicals produced on a smaller scale are called fine chemicals. Examples of these include:
   - Speciality chemicals — e.g. some medicines.
   - Dyes — soluble chemicals used in colouring, e.g. dyes are used to colour clothes.
   - Pigments — insoluble chemicals used in colouring, e.g. pigments are used to colour paint.
2) Many fine chemicals require several different production stages.

Fine chemicals — by appointment to Her Majesty, The Queen...

We humans use loads of different types of chemical products each day, e.g. a farmer might spread fertiliser on his fields or a pharmacist might give out medicines to a customer. These chemicals are made on a large or small scale depending on how they're used, e.g. loads of fertiliser is used in farming so it's produced on a large scale.

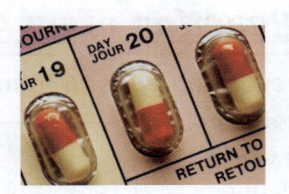

Unit 2: Topic 4 — Making Chemical Products

Acids and Alkalis

Chemicals (including those in your kitchen, or garden shed) can be acidic, alkaline or neutral.

pH is a Measure of Acidity or Alkalinity

The acidity (or alkalinity) of a chemical is measured on the pH scale.

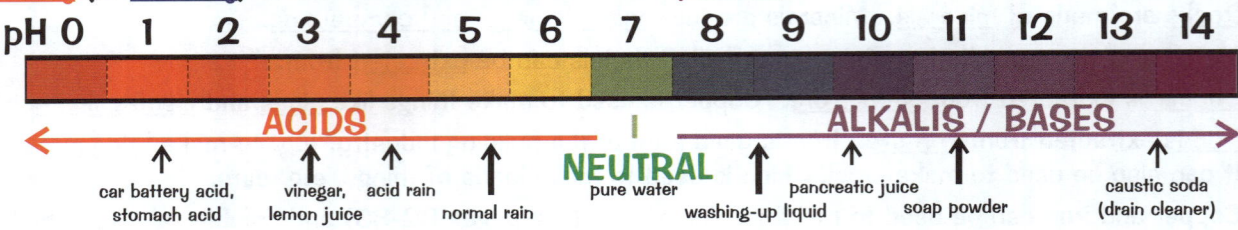

pH 0 1 2 3 4 5 6 7 8 9 10 11 12 13 14

← ACIDS | ALKALIS / BASES →

NEUTRAL

car battery acid, stomach acid — vinegar, lemon juice — acid rain — normal rain — pure water — washing-up liquid — pancreatic juice — soap powder — caustic soda (drain cleaner)

1) An acid is a chemical with a pH below 7.
2) A base is a chemical with a pH above 7. Bases that dissolve are called alkalis.
   E.g. ammonia gas is a base. Ammonia in solution is an alkali.
   Metal oxides and hydroxides are also bases (the ones that dissolve are alkalis).
3) Solutions that are neither acids nor alkalis are called neutral, and have a pH of exactly 7.
4) A solution's pH can be measured with a pH meter (like the one on the right) or by adding Universal Indicator to the solution. Universal Indicator is a combination of dyes, and gives the colours in the pH scale shown above.

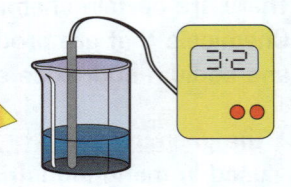

Acids and Bases Can Be Produced from Raw Materials

Raw materials are the simple starting materials used to make a product. Chemical products are made from simple chemicals, for example:

1) Ammonia is made from nitrogen (from the air) and hydrogen (from natural gas or crude oil).

2) Sulfuric acid is made from sulfur (found in rocks), oxygen (from the air) and water.

3) Sodium hydroxide is made from sodium chloride (salt) solution (salt is found in underground deposits).

You know that ammonia is a base, as is sodium hydroxide. Sulfuric acid is... you guessed it, an acid.

The Reaction of an Acid with an Alkali is Called Neutralisation

Alkalis react with acids to form neutral ionic compounds called salts, plus water.
This equation is really worth remembering:

ACID + ALKALI → SALT + WATER
E.g. hydrochloric acid + sodium hydroxide → sodium chloride + water
(an acid) (an alkali) (a salt)

This kind of reaction is called neutralisation, since the pH of the salt solution is 7.
Salts produced by the neutralisation reactions of ammonia and sulfuric acid are often used in fertilisers.

Neutral — I don't mind either way...

Neutralisation is a reaction that you'll find popping up time and time again — it doesn't just go on in the lab or during large-scale chemical synthesis. Taking indigestion tablets causes a neutralisation reaction in your stomach. The tablets contain a base that neutralises excess hydrochloric acid and makes you feel better. Lovely.

Unit 2: Topic 4 — Making Chemical Products

Reactions of Acids

I'm afraid there's more stuff on neutralisation reactions coming up...

Metal Oxides and Metal Hydroxides React with Acids

1) Metal oxides and metal hydroxides that dissolve in water are alkalis (see previous page).
2) So, all metal oxides and metal hydroxides react with acids to form a salt and water.

$$\text{ACID} + \text{METAL OXIDE} \rightarrow \text{SALT} + \text{WATER}$$

$$\text{ACID} + \text{METAL HYDROXIDE} \rightarrow \text{SALT} + \text{WATER}$$

(These are neutralisation reactions of course)

The Name of the Salt Depends on What's Reacting

The name of the salt produced in a neutralisation reaction depends on the acid and alkali used. Take a look at the examples below.

1) Hydrochloric acid produces chloride salts. Here are some examples:

   hydrochloric acid + zinc oxide → zinc chloride + water
   hydrochloric acid + sodium hydroxide → sodium chloride + water

2) Nitric acid produces nitrate salts. Have a look at these:

   nitric acid + magnesium oxide → magnesium nitrate + water
   nitric acid + potassium hydroxide → potassium nitrate + water

3) Sulfuric acid produces sulfate salts. You guessed it — here are two more examples:

   sulfuric acid + copper(II) oxide → copper(II) sulfate + water
   sulfuric acid + magnesium hydroxide → magnesium sulfate + water

The first part of a salt's name comes from the alkali. The second part comes from the acid.

Acid + Metal → Salt + Hydrogen

Here's another one of those really important equations. Learn it...

$$\text{ACID} + \text{METAL} \rightarrow \text{SALT} + \text{HYDROGEN}$$

You can see this reaction happening if you put a small volume of hydrochloric acid into a test tube and add a piece of magnesium. You'll see little bubbles of gas rising to the surface — that's hydrogen.

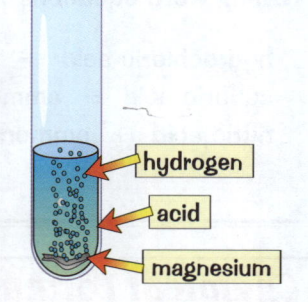

Naming the salt is done in exactly the same way as above. Just follow these rules...

Hydrochloric acid will always produce **chloride salts**
hydrochloric acid + magnesium → magnesium chloride + hydrogen

The first part of the salt's name is the metal. The second part comes from the acid.

Sulfuric acid will always produce **sulfate salts**
sulfuric acid + zinc → zinc sulfate + hydrogen

Nitric acid will always produce **nitrate salts**
nitric acid + iron → iron nitrate + hydrogen

Examples of salts — salt on my chips, salt on my crisps...

Salts have many uses — they're used in everything from food to medicines. So get learning how to make them.

Unit 2: Topic 4 — Making Chemical Products

Reactions of Acids and Chemical Formulae

You also need to know about the reactions of acids with metal carbonates and ammonia. These reactions are similar to the ones on the previous page — they each make a salt.

Acid + Metal Carbonate → Salt + Water + Carbon Dioxide

Again, this reaction produces a salt, but this time, carbon dioxide and water are produced too.

ACID + METAL CARBONATE → SALT + WATER + CARBON DIOXIDE

Writing equations for these reactions is just as easy as it was for acid-metal reactions.

Hydrochloric acid will always produce chloride salts

hydrochloric acid + magnesium carbonate → magnesium chloride + water + carbon dioxide
hydrochloric acid + zinc carbonate → zinc chloride + water + carbon dioxide

Sulfuric acid will always produce sulfate salts

sulfuric acid + magnesium carbonate → magnesium sulfate + water + carbon dioxide
sulfuric acid + zinc carbonate → zinc sulfate + water + carbon dioxide

Nitric acid will always produce nitrate salts

nitric acid + zinc carbonate → zinc nitrate + water + carbon dioxide
nitric acid + calcium carbonate → calcium nitrate + water + carbon dioxide

Ammonia + Acid → Salt

If you're getting the hang of this page then you'll have guessed that when ammonia reacts with acid, yep, a salt is made. Learn this:

ACID + AMMONIA → SALT

Writing word equations for this reaction is easy peasy, for example:

hydrochloric acid + ammonia → ammonium chloride
sulfuric acid + ammonia → ammonium sulphate
nitric acid + ammonia → ammonium nitrate

The first part of the salt's name is always 'ammonium'. The second part comes from the acid.

Chemical Formulae Show the Atoms in a Substance

'Formulae' is the plural of 'formula'.

You can work out how many atoms of each type there are in a substance when you're given its formula. Here are some examples:

This is called a chemical formula. It shows the number and type of atoms in a molecule.

CO_2 — Carbon dioxide contains 1 carbon atom and 2 oxygen atoms.

H_2O — Water contains 2 hydrogen atoms and 1 oxygen atom.

Kettle + acid → tea + stomach ache...

If you've ever descaled a kettle, you'll know that there's a lot of fizzing. That's actually an acid (the descaler) reacting with a carbonate (the scale) — the fizzing is the carbon dioxide escaping. Make sure you know the overall equations for metal oxides, metal hydroxides, metals, metal carbonates and ammonia reacting with acids.

Unit 2: Topic 4 — Making Chemical Products

Solutions

Many chemical products are solutions. And when it comes to solutions, concentration is really important...

A Solution Means a Solute is Dissolved in a Solvent

1) A solution is a mixture of a solute and a solvent.
2) The solute is the thing (often a solid) being dissolved, and the solvent is the liquid it dissolves in. For example, when you dissolve salt in water, salt is the solute and water is the solvent.
3) The concentration of a solution tells you how much solute is dissolved in a volume of solution. There's an easy formula:

$$\text{concentration} = \frac{\text{mass (of solute)}}{\text{volume (of solution)}}$$

Remember: 1 cm^3 = 1 ml
1 litre = 1000 cm^3 (or 1000 ml)

4) Concentration is usually measured in: g/cm^3 — grams of solute per cm^3 of solution.
   or: g/litre (g/l) — grams of solute per litre of solution.

Making a Solution of Known Concentration

Scientists working in labs (e.g. in hospitals or chemical analysis centres) need to know how to make solutions of particular concentrations. You might have to do this too. So here's how...

Example: Describe how to make 0.5 litres of sodium chloride solution with a concentration of 30 g/l.

First, the theory: You know that one litre of solution would contain 30 g of sodium chloride. So 0.5 litres of solution would need half this amount — 15 g.

Next, the practice: First things first — check whether there are any hazards associated with sodium chloride, and make sure you take any necessary precautions.

1) Add 15 g of sodium chloride (the solute) to a graduated flask.
2) Add some distilled water (the solvent) to the flask and then stir until all the sodium chloride has dissolved.
3) Add some more distilled water to make up the volume to the exact amount you need (0.5 litres).

This is a standard procedure (see p.92).

One important thing here... you mustn't start with 0.5 litres of water and add 15 g of sodium chloride. This will make the total volume a little bit more than 0.5 litres. Which isn't what you want.

Use the Concentration Formula to find Mass

You can rearrange the concentration formula to get: **mass = concentration × volume**

Example: How many grams of sodium chloride are in 400 cm^3 of a 0.25 g/cm^3 solution?
Answer: Mass = concentration × volume = 0.25 × 400 = 100 g

Example: How many grams of calcium chloride are in 2000 cm^3 of a 4 g/litre solution?
Answer: Be very careful with the units — you've got volume in cm^3, but concentration in g/litre. So, convert everything to litres first. Volume = 2000 cm^3 = 2 litres. This means that... mass = concentration × volume = 4 × 2 = 8 grams

Learning this takes some mental concentration...

With orange squash, you can just keep adding water till it tastes about right. You can't do that in GCSE Additional Applied Science — because the solution you're making might well be poisonous, and because the concentration has to be spot on, not just 'about right'. So measure everything very carefully, then it'll be perfect.

Unit 2: Topic 4 — Making Chemical Products

Making Insoluble Salts

Insoluble chemicals are chemicals that don't dissolve. They're often made by mixing two solutions. In the lab, you do the mixing in a beaker. In industry, you might use a container the size of a house.

Insoluble Chemicals are Produced by Precipitation Reactions

1) In a precipitation reaction, two solutions are mixed together to form an insoluble product.
2) The insoluble substance formed is called a precipitate — it turns the solution cloudy because it doesn't dissolve (this usually happens pretty quickly).
3) Suppose you want to make some copper(II) carbonate — a blue-green salt. One way to do this is to mix together a solution of copper(II) nitrate and a solution of sodium carbonate.

> Put one solution into a small beaker and carefully add the other solution.

> Give it a good stir to make sure it's all mixed together.

> A blue-green substance will form immediately — this is the precipitate.

You Need to be Able to Write Equations for Precipitation Reactions

You need to be able to write word equations for the formation of insoluble salts from two solutions. Here's the equation for the copper(II) carbonate reaction described above:

> copper(II) nitrate + sodium carbonate → copper(II) carbonate + sodium nitrate
> (solution)   (solution)   (precipitate)   (solution)

Notice how the different bits of the reactants basically just "swap partners".

Insoluble Salts Have Many Different Uses

Insoluble salts can be used as pigments (see page 77) in paints and cosmetics. Copper(II) carbonate is used as a pigment. So is cobalt phosphate (another insoluble salt). Cobalt phosphate can be made using this precipitation reaction:

> potassium phosphate + cobalt chloride → cobalt phosphate + potassium chloride

Magnesium carbonate and calcium carbonate are insoluble salts used in health products. Here's how they can be made:

> magnesium nitrate + sodium carbonate → magnesium carbonate + sodium nitrate

> calcium chloride + sodium carbonate → calcium carbonate + sodium chloride

Precipitation — I thought that was rain...

So, insoluble salts can be made by reacting two solutions together. In the exam, you could be asked to write a word equation for this kind of reaction — and it might involve two solutions you've not seen before. Don't panic, just remember that the reactants swap partners (as above). And one of the products will be a precipitate.

Unit 2: Topic 4 — Making Chemical Products

Making Insoluble Salts

If you've mixed two solutions together in a beaker to make an insoluble salt, the beaker will now contain a precipitate of the salt and a solution. Not that helpful. So here's what you do next...

Insoluble Chemicals are Separated First by Filtering...

Because it's insoluble, the precipitate can be separated from the solution by filtering.

1) Put a folded piece of filter paper into a filter funnel and stick the funnel into a conical flask.

2) Pour the contents of the beaker into the middle of the filter paper. (Make sure that the solution doesn't go above the filter paper — otherwise some of the solid could dribble down the side.)

3) Swill out the beaker with distilled water and tip this into the filter paper — to make sure you get all the product from the beaker.

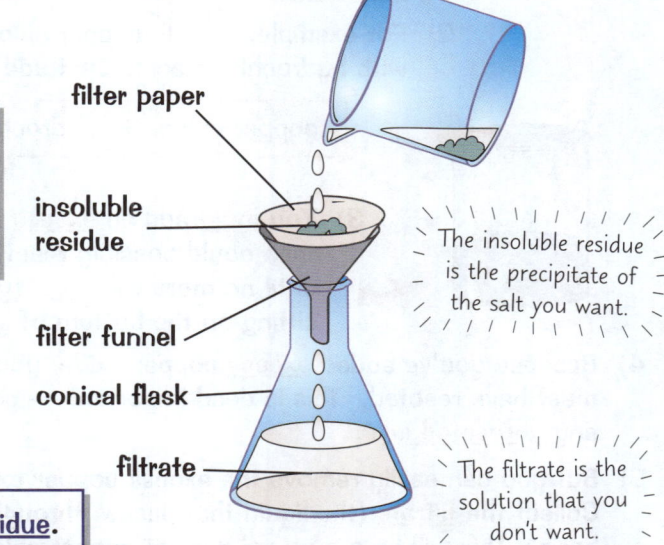

4) The solid left in the filter paper is the insoluble residue.

5) The liquid that collects in the conical flask is called the filtrate.

The insoluble residue is the precipitate of the salt you want.

The filtrate is the solution that you don't want.

...and then by Drying

Chances are, the insoluble salt on your filter paper will be a bit impure (and soggy).

1) First you need to rinse the contents of the filter paper with distilled water to make sure that all the soluble compounds have been washed away. Then just scrape the insoluble salt onto some fresh filter paper.

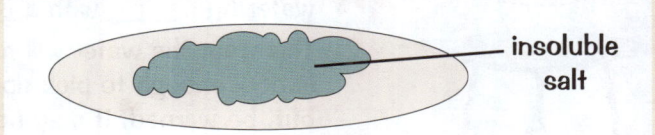

2) Now you need to dry it. There are a couple of different ways of drying the product. It can simply be left on the side to dry, but many industrial laboratories have ovens used for drying chemicals, and others have desiccators — pots that contain chemicals that absorb the water from other substances.

It can all be quite dull — like watching chemicals dry...

Insoluble chemicals are pretty simple to separate out — just remember to filter, rinse and dry. You need to rinse the precipitate to get rid of any of the filtrate that is left on it, so you end up with a pure insoluble salt. What more could any chemist want — so if you know a chemist and need to get them a present, there you go...

Unit 2: Topic 4 — Making Chemical Products

Making Soluble Salts

If the salt you're trying to get is soluble (it dissolves), then there's no way you're going to be able to separate it from the solution using filtration. This time, you need to use evaporation and crystallisation...

Add an Excess of the Insoluble Reactant

This technique involves mixing a soluble substance with an insoluble one to give a soluble product.

1) Because your product is soluble, you can't separate it out by filtration. But, you can use filtration to remove any insoluble reactant left over — that's the idea here.

2) For example, soluble copper chloride is made by reacting insoluble copper oxide with hydrochloric acid. Just add copper oxide powder to some hydrochloric acid.

copper oxide + hydrochloric acid → copper chloride + water
base + acid → salt + water

3) You must add an excess of the insoluble reactant (i.e. more than could possibly react). Keep adding more and stirring until no more will react (you must see bits of copper oxide sitting on the bottom of your beaker).

4) Because you've added excess copper oxide, you know all the hydrochloric acid must have reacted. This is dead important — you'd have a helluva job removing any unreacted acid.

5) But you can easily remove the excess copper oxide — by filtration (see page 83). Collect the filtrate (the liquid that passes through the filter paper) in an evaporating basin. This will be a pure solution of copper chloride. It's a good idea to rinse the residue and filter paper with distilled water to make sure you've got all the product.

Evaporation and Crystallisation Produce a Solid Product

Your next job is to get rid of the solvent (water) — this will leave you with pure, solid copper chloride. If some of the water is removed, so that there is not enough to dissolve the product completely, solid particles called crystals will form — this is known as crystallisation. Removing more water causes more solid to form. The solid left after the water has gone is called the residue.

Water can be removed by evaporation — where the liquid water turns into a vapour and drifts away:

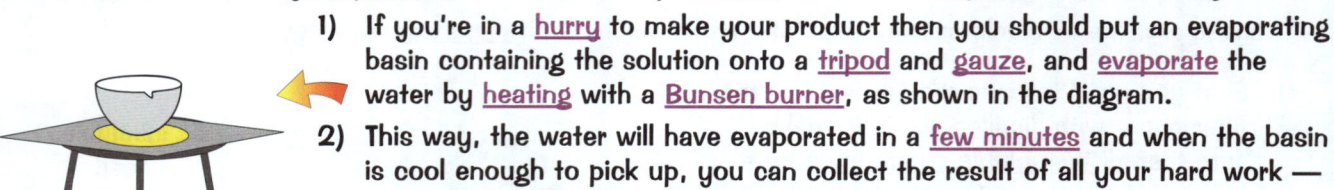

1) If you're in a hurry to make your product then you should put an evaporating basin containing the solution onto a tripod and gauze, and evaporate the water by heating with a Bunsen burner, as shown in the diagram.

2) This way, the water will have evaporated in a few minutes and when the basin is cool enough to pick up, you can collect the result of all your hard work — but, be warned, it may not look very impressive.

3) This is because most crystals grow quite slowly, so a rapid crystallisation like this produces lots of little crystals.

4) If you want to make really big crystals then you'll have to wait for the water to evaporate slowly.

Soluble Salts have Many Different Uses

Examples of soluble salts include:
- Zinc sulfate — used in dietary supplements for people who are lacking in zinc.
- Iron(II) sulfate — used in dietary supplements for people who are lacking in iron.
- Magnesium sufate — used in bath salts.
- Copper (II) sulfate — used in agriculture as a fungicide (see page 61).

Unit 2: Topic 4 — Making Chemical Products

Neutralising an Acid

Here's the last method you'll need to know about for producing a pure salt.
It's the trickiest of the lot — this is because your reactants and product are all soluble.

Titrations Can Be Used to Produce a Pure Salt

When your reactants and product are all soluble, you can't get rid of anything by filtering. And it's no good adding an excess of anything — you'd struggle to get rid of it later. So what you have to do is add just the right amount of each reactant. For example, in an acid-base titration, you need to add just the right amounts of acid and alkali.

1) When a soluble salt is made by reacting an acid with an alkali, it's important that exactly the right amount of each is added — so that the final solution contains only the salt and water.

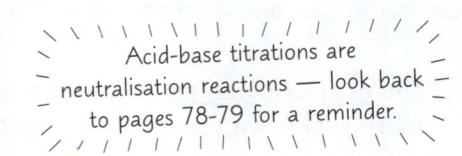

   Acid-base titrations are neutralisation reactions — look back to pages 78-79 for a reminder.

2) This is done by carefully mixing a suitable acid and alkali until the pH is 7. You can use the titration apparatus shown in the diagram.

3) For example, if you wanted to produce sodium chloride, you could titrate hydrochloric acid with sodium hydroxide:
   hydrochloric acid + sodium hydroxide → sodium chloride + water

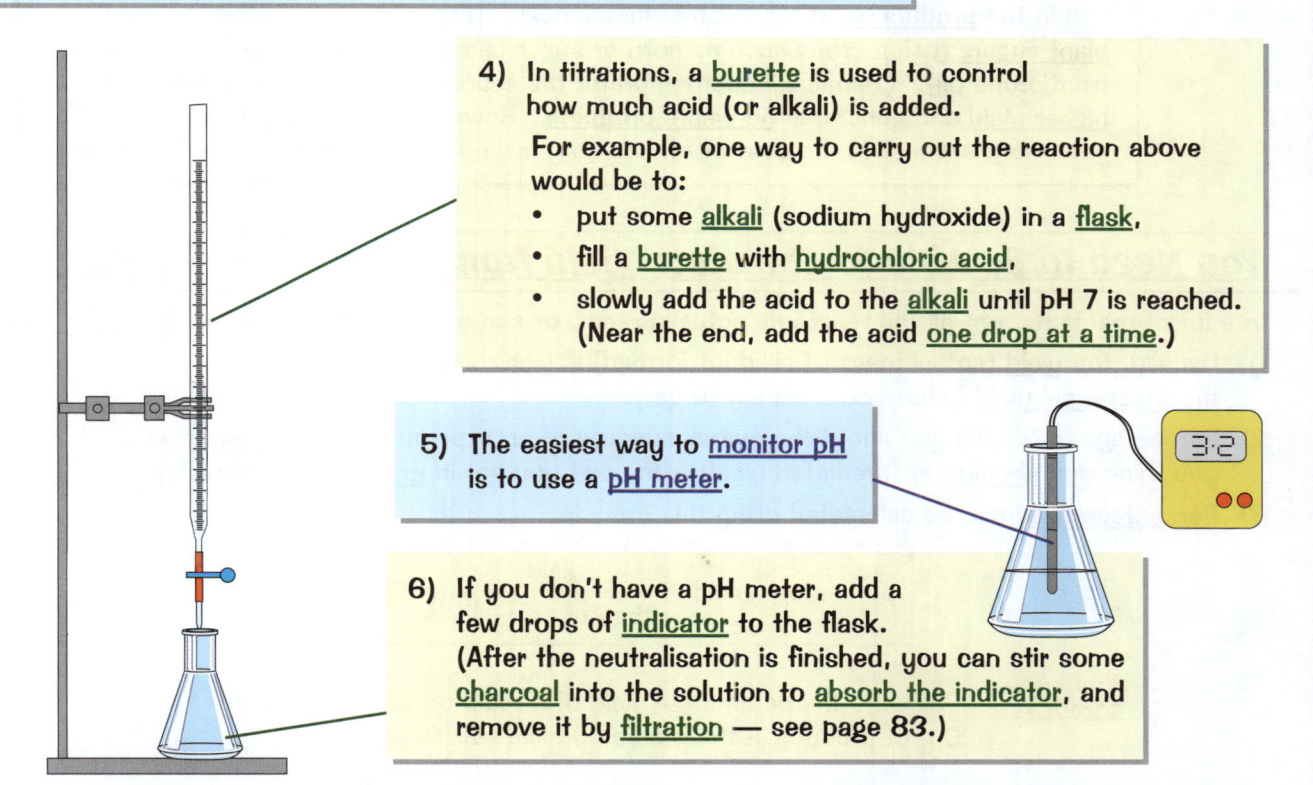

4) In titrations, a burette is used to control how much acid (or alkali) is added.
   For example, one way to carry out the reaction above would be to:
   - put some alkali (sodium hydroxide) in a flask,
   - fill a burette with hydrochloric acid,
   - slowly add the acid to the alkali until pH 7 is reached. (Near the end, add the acid one drop at a time.)

5) The easiest way to monitor pH is to use a pH meter.

6) If you don't have a pH meter, add a few drops of indicator to the flask. (After the neutralisation is finished, you can stir some charcoal into the solution to absorb the indicator, and remove it by filtration — see page 83.)

7) Crystals of the pure salt can be made by evaporating the water in the same way as on page 84.

Pure salt — I prefer salt and vinegar...

There are different ways of obtaining your solid product depending on whether it's soluble or insoluble. You could be asked to describe how you'd obtain a sample of a certain salt, and you'd need to be able to choose the right method depending on its solubility. So make sure you've got all this stuff learnt — it'll be worth it in the exam.

Unit 2: Topic 4 — Making Chemical Products

Chemical Synthesis and Yields

Before a company begins building a plant to produce a chemical, a lot of research has to be done to find the optimum method of chemical synthesis — the best way of making the product...

There's Usually More Than One Method to Make a Chemical

To make a particular chemical, scientists have to decide which reaction (or sequence of reactions) to use. Often there are several methods that can be used to make the same product. Before deciding which to use, scientists will want to know many things, such as...

1) The yield (the actual mass of product formed by the reaction) — if this is too low the reaction will be wasteful and expensive.

2) The cost of materials — some reactions may require more expensive chemicals or equipment than others.

3) How much energy will be needed — maintaining high temperatures can burn a lot of fuel, which is expensive and creates pollution.

4) What the waste products are — if a reaction produces dangerous waste it can be very expensive to dispose of or to recycle.

Ethanol is an important industrial chemical used as a fuel, a solvent, an antiseptic, and in the production of many other substances. It's currently produced either from plant sugars (using crops such as corn or sugar cane) or from ethene (which comes from crude oil). Chemical industries prefer the second method because it gives a higher yield and generates no waste products. However, in the future, as crude oil gets more expensive, the cost of ethene may make it unprofitable to use this method.

You Need to Be Able to Calculate Yield from Experimental Data

In a lot of reactions, not all the reactants actually react, or some of the product is lost along the way.

1) Usually, the yield (actual mass of product formed) is less than the theoretical yield (what you'd expect to get).
2) Percentage yield tells you about the overall success of an experiment. It compares what you think you should get (predicted yield) with what you get in practice (actual yield).
3) Percentage yield can be calculated using this formula:

$$\text{percentage yield} = \frac{\text{yield}}{\text{theoretical yield}} \times 100$$

EXAMPLE: Calculate the percentage yield of a reaction which produced 9 g of product, if the predicted yield was 15 g.

ANSWER: $\text{percentage yield} = \frac{\text{yield}}{\text{theoretical yield}} \times 100 = \frac{9}{15} \times 100 = \underline{60\%}$

Revision yield depends on the amount of biscuits eaten and tea drunk...

There are loads of factors that influence a company's choice of method when producing chemicals. Even though you produce the same thing, different methods use different amounts of energy, produce different waste products, cost different amounts and give different yields. Plenty to be weighed up in your big, juicy brain.

Unit 2: Topic 4 — Making Chemical Products

Rates of Reaction

It's important to be able to control and measure the rate of chemical reactions, especially in industry.

Reactions Can Go at All Sorts of Different Rates

The rate of a chemical reaction is how fast the reactants are changed into products — the reaction is over when one of the reactants is completely used up.

1) One of the slowest is the rusting of iron (it's not slow enough though — what about my little Mini).
2) A moderate speed reaction is a metal (like magnesium) reacting with acid to produce a gentle stream of bubbles.
3) A really fast reaction is an explosion, where it's all over in a fraction of a second.

Three Ways to Measure the Rate of a Reaction

The rate (speed) of a reaction can be observed either by how quickly the reactants are used up or how quickly the products are formed. It's usually a lot easier to measure products forming. The rate of reaction can be calculated using the following equation:

$$\text{Rate of Reaction} = \frac{\text{Amount of reactant used or amount of product formed}}{\text{Time}}$$

There are different ways that the rate of a reaction can be measured. Have a look at these three:

1) PRECIPITATION

1) This is when the product of the reaction is a precipitate, which makes the solution cloudy.
2) Observe a marker through the solution and measure how long it takes for it to disappear.
3) The quicker the marker disappears, the quicker the reaction.

2) CHANGE IN MASS (USUALLY GAS GIVEN OFF)

1) Measuring the speed of a reaction that produces a gas can be carried out on a mass balance.
2) As the gas is released, the mass disappearing is measured on the balance.
3) The quicker the reading on the balance drops, the faster the reaction.

3) THE VOLUME OF GAS GIVEN OFF

1) This involves the use of a gas syringe to measure the volume of gas given off.
2) The more gas given off during a given time interval, the faster the reaction.
3) A graph of gas volume against time could be plotted to give a rate of reaction graph.

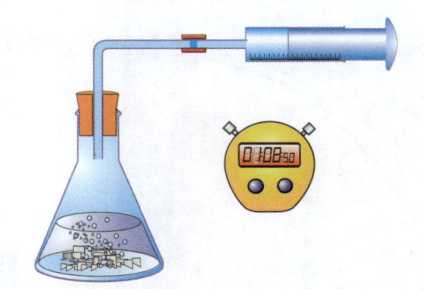

OK have you got your stopwatch ready *BANG!* — oh...

Each of the three methods described above have their pros and cons. The mass balance method is only accurate as long as the flask isn't too hot, otherwise you lose mass by evaporation as well as by the reaction. The first method isn't very accurate, but if you're not producing a gas you can't use either of the other two. Ah well.

Unit 2: Topic 4 — Making Chemical Products

Rates of Reaction

As well as being able to measure the rate of a reaction, scientists in the chemical industry also need to know the things that affect the rate. This helps them get the optimum conditions for a reaction.

The Rate of a Reaction Depends on Four Things

1) TEMPERATURE — As the temperature increases, the rate of reaction increases.
2) CONCENTRATION — Increasing the concentration of the reactants increases the rate of reaction.
3) SIZE OF PARTICLES — The smaller the particles the faster the rate of reaction.
4) CATALYST — Using a catalyst increases the rate of reaction. A catalyst is a substance that changes the speed of a reaction, without being changed or used up in the reaction.

That's all very nice. But in the exam they might ask you to interpret rate-of-reaction data. Read on...

Changing Any of These Factors Alters the Reaction Rate Graph

The graph opposite shows how the rate of a particular reaction varies under different conditions. The quickest reaction is shown by the line that becomes flat in the least time.

1) Graph 1 represents the original reaction.
2) Graphs 2 and 3 represent the reaction taking place quicker, but with the same initial amounts. The same amount of product is produced overall — just at a quicker rate.
3) The increased rate could be due to any of these:

   a) increase in temperature
   b) increase in concentration
   c) solid reactant crushed up into smaller bits
   d) catalyst added

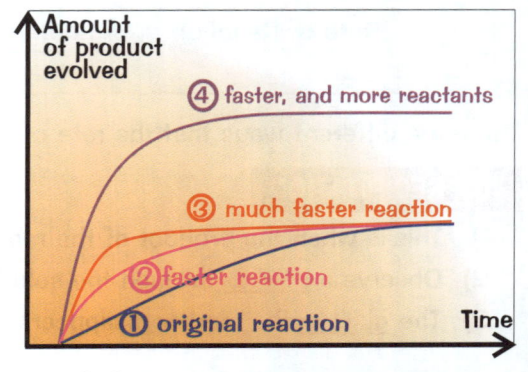

4) Graph 4 produces more product as well as going faster. This can only happen if more reactant(s) are added at the start. Graphs 1, 2 and 3 all converge at the same level, showing that they all produce the same amount of product, although they take different times to get there.

You've Got to be Able to Read Rate of Reaction Graphs

In this experiment, some marble chips were added to a solution of hydrochloric acid. Any gases released were collected using a gas syringe (see p.87) — the volume was recorded every 10 s.

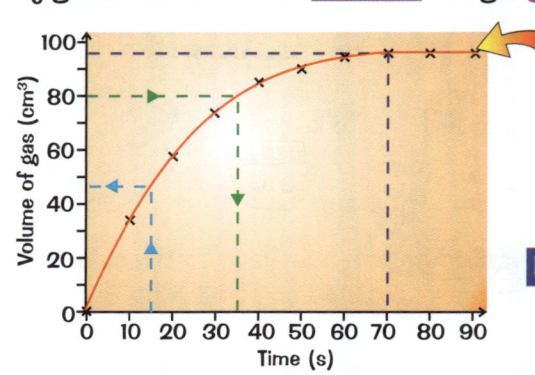

The results are shown on this graph.

1) The total volume of gas produced is 96 cm³.
2) The reaction had stopped after about 70 s — no more gas was produced (so the line on the graph was horizontal).

Examples: How much gas was produced after 15 s? 47 cm³
How long did it take to produce 80 cm³ of gas? 35 s

Easy.

My reactions slow down when it gets hot — I get sleepy...

Reaction rate depends on four factors. See if you can list them without looking — they're all on this page.

Unit 2: Topic 4 — Making Chemical Products

Mixtures

Loads of everyday things are mixtures of some kind, where one substance is finely dispersed in another. For example, paints, cosmetics, medicines and food and drink. Read on...

An Emulsion is a Cloudy Mixture of a Liquid in Another Liquid

1) An emulsion is made from tiny droplets of one liquid dispersed in another, where the liquids won't dissolve in each other, e.g. oil and water.
2) Emulsion paint, mayonnaise and some salad dressings are examples of emulsions.
3) Emulsions are made by slowly adding the two liquids together whilst beating the mixture continuously (nonstop).
4) Emulsions are cloudy, and will eventually separate if left for a while. For example:

You can make salad dressing from olive oil and vinegar. You shake it up to make a cloudy liquid then drench your lettuce with it. But if you come back to it tomorrow lunchtime, the oil will have separated out and be sitting on top of the vinegar, so you'll have to shake it up again.

5) To stop an emulsion from separating, you can add an emulsifier (or emulsifying agent) to it. Emulsifiers are molecules that help the two liquids in an emulsion stay mixed together.
6) Emulsions are useful because their properties are different from the properties of their ingredients.

Examples:
- Mayonnaise is an emulsion of sunflower oil (or olive oil) and vinegar — it's thicker than either and so easier to spread.
- A salad dressing made by shaking olive oil and vinegar together forms an emulsion that coats salad better than plain oil or plain vinegar.
- Most moisturising lotions are oil-in-water emulsions. The smooth texture of an emulsion makes it easy to rub into the skin.

A Suspension is a Cloudy Mixture of a Solid in a Liquid

1) A suspension is a mixture of small solid particles (e.g. silt) mixed in with a liquid (e.g. water).
2) The particles don't mix completely — they don't dissolve and there are no chemical bonds.
3) The particles aren't small enough to stay floating around — eventually they will separate, and the solid particles gradually settle to the bottom.

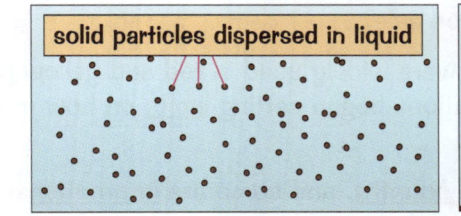

4) Muddy water is a great example of a suspension — get a jar of muddy water, leave it on the side for an hour or two, and you'll end up with clear water with a layer of sludge at the bottom. Nice.
5) Ice cream is another example — tiny crystals of ice suspended in cream.

Who knew lunch involved quite as much chemistry...

Finally, an excuse to eat tonnes of ice cream — you can tell yourself it's ground-breaking research into particulate bonding in suspensions. And you wouldn't want to hinder your educational development now would you...

Unit 2: Topic 4 — Making Chemical Products

Testing Formulations

Companies are constantly testing their products in quality control procedures to make sure that they're performing as they should and are safe for customers to use.

Testing is an Important Part of Quality Assurance

To make sure that a product is always of the same quality, regular reports about its purity, chemical composition and physical properties will be written based on the results of tests. If the properties of a substance are not the same each time the tests are done, engineers will investigate why this is, and may make changes to the way in which the product is made. This process of checking and improving the manufacturing process is called quality assurance.

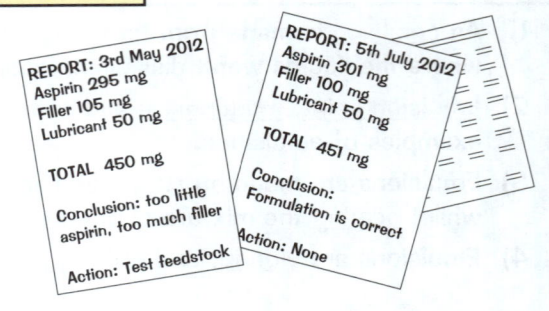

REPORT: 3rd May 2012
Aspirin 295 mg
Filler 105 mg
Lubricant 50 mg
TOTAL 450 mg
Conclusion: too little aspirin, too much filler
Action: Test feedstock

REPORT: 5th July 2012
Aspirin 301 mg
Filler 100 mg
Lubricant 50 mg
TOTAL 451 mg
Conclusion: Formulation is correct
Action: None

Testing is Necessary for Consumer Protection

There are laws in nearly all countries to ensure that when you buy a chemical product you're getting what you pay for. Companies must test their products to make sure they do the job they're meant to do and are not going to harm consumers. For example, washing powders will be tested to see if they clean clothes properly and also to make sure that they do not cause any skin reactions.

Example: Two new chemicals, A and B, designed to be stain removers are put through a series of tests.

	chemical A	chemical B
stains removed (out of 100)	98	43
skin reactions in patch tests	some irritation	no reactions

Neither of the chemicals is very suitable. A isn't safe (it causes skin irritation) and B isn't very effective (it removes less than half of the 100 different stains). However, chemical A could be used in industrial cleaners that are used by trained staff wearing protective gloves.

Products Must Meet National and International Standards

1) As well as companies testing their own products, there are national laboratories whose job it is to check that chemical products meet certain standards set by governments.

2) National laboratories randomly test chemical products that are on sale, and if they find a company is not meeting standards then that company will have to stop selling its product and can be fined a lot of money. To make sure this doesn't happen, companies do their own testing to prevent any of their products that don't comply with the standards from going on sale.

3) Cadmium compounds were widely used in red and yellow paints. In 1998 the United Nations began setting limits on how much cadmium was allowed.

4) Some of these standards are enforced within one country, and some are international standards that all companies must comply with. For instance, different countries around the world allow different levels of lead additive in petrol. Many countries have banned lead altogether. So some petrol formulations are illegal to sell in one country but not in another.

Checking and improving — sounds like revision to me...

It might seem like a lot of time and effort, but it's really important that products are regularly checked and tested, especially if they contain chemicals that could be harmful in the wrong amounts. Don't have nightmares folks.

Unit 2: Topic 4 — Making Chemical Products

Revision Summary

You've covered quite a lot in this section. So here are some questions to test yourself with. I know — just what you always wanted... If you can't remember something, it's really important that you check back through the section. Don't just ignore it — it could be something that comes up in the exam.

1) Give three things that a lab technician's role includes.
2) At a chemical plant, explain what a finance officer does.
3) Give three types of facilities a chemical plant needs nearby.
4) Give two reasons why governments regulate the manufacture and use of chemicals.
5) What is the Health and Safety Executive responsible for?
6) What is a risk assessment?
7) What can you tell about a chemical from each of the following hazchem symbols?
   a)   b)   c)
8) Name two metals that need to be extracted from their ores.
9) What is the difference between a bulk chemical and a fine chemical?
10) Give one use of ammonia.
11) Give two examples of fine chemicals.
12) What are alkalis?
13) What are the raw materials needed for making: a) ammonia, b) sodium hydroxide?
14)* Write a word equation to show the reaction between sodium hydroxide and nitric acid.
15)* Write a word equation to show the reaction between calcium carbonate and hydrochloric acid.
16) How many carbon atoms are in carbon dioxide — CO_2?
17)* How many grams of sodium chloride are in 600 cm^3 of a 0.5 g/cm^3 solution?
18) Write a word equation to show the precipitation reaction between copper(II) nitrate and sodium carbonate.
19) You're mixing two solutions to form a precipitate of copper(II) carbonate. Explain how you would separate and dry the precipitate.
20) When making a soluble salt from an insoluble chemical and an acid, why is it important that the insoluble solid is added until no more will react?
21) Explain how you'd produce a solid salt from a solution using evaporation and crystallisation.
22) If you were producing a pure salt by the neutralisation of two soluble chemicals, how would you ensure that the final solution only contained the salt?
23) Give three factors that might influence the choice of method for making a chemical in industry.
24)* A reaction's yield is 40 tonnes and its theoretical yield is 52 tonnes. Calculate the percentage yield.
25) Give one method for measuring the rate of a reaction.
26) What four things does the rate of a reaction depend on?
27)* Look at this rate of reaction graph. How long did it take for the reaction to complete?
28) What is an emulsion? Give an example of an emulsion found in the home.
29) What is a suspension?
30) Explain why products must be routinely checked.

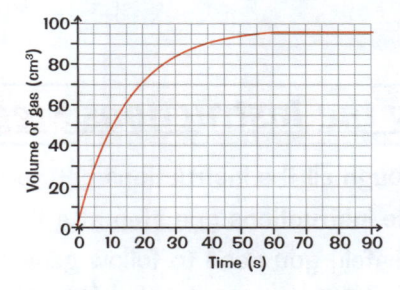

* Answers on p. 108.

Unit 2: Topic 4 — Making Chemical Products

Unit 3 — Controlled Assessment

Standard Procedures

For your controlled assessment, you'll have to complete a work-related portfolio. This will be made up of four standard procedures, one suitability test and one work-related report — the next few pages will give you some advice about all of them. First up though, standard procedures...

Standard Procedures Help Ensure Results are Reliable

Standard procedures are agreed methods of working that scientists use to make sure their results are reliable and of a good quality.

For example, a standard procedure is used to culture (grow) a sample of bacteria on an agar plate (a Petri dish containing agar jelly).

There are six things you need to do to follow a standard procedure properly...

Example: Standard procedure for culturing bacteria.

1) Measure out 1 cm³ of culture solution into a sterile sample bottle.
2) Spread the 1 cm³ of culture solution over an agar plate using a sterile swab.
3) Seal the agar plate with sticky tape and label it.
4) Incubate the agar plate for 48 hours.
5) Count the number of colonies and measure their area to the nearest mm², using graph paper.
6) Find the average area of the colonies produced.

1) Write a Risk Assessment

You'll need to write a risk assessment for each standard procedure. This involves:

1) Identifying any hazards (things that could cause harm).
2) Describing the risk of each of these hazards.
3) Suggesting a suitable way to reduce each risk.
4) Stating what should be done in the case of an accident.
5) Stating whether the procedure as a whole is low risk or high risk.

Try to think of all the risks, not just the obvious ones.*

Example: Risk assessment for culturing bacteria.

This standard procedure is fairly low risk. There are not many hazards involved. By following normal lab safety rules and my risk assessment, there should be no problems.

Hazard	Risk involved	How to reduce risk	In case of an accident
Using glass equipment	Glass breaking causing cuts.	Take care handling glass. Report any breakages immediately.	Tell a teacher and a first aider. Minor cuts should be washed and bandaged. More serious injuries might need further treatment.
Bacteria	Contamination of people or environment with bacteria.	Avoid hand to mouth/eye contact. Wear protective clothing. Wash hands after experiment. Use aseptic techniques. Don't open culture dishes once sealed. Dispose of cultures safely.	Tell a teacher. In the case of an accidental spill, clean the contaminated area thoroughly.

Make sure you use the correct scientific terms in your risk assessment wherever you can, e.g. 'aseptic techniques'.

2) Follow the Instructions Step By Step

1) Read through all the instructions before you begin — make sure you understand absolutely everything.
2) Follow the instructions one step at a time, making sure you don't miss out any steps.
3) To work safely you need to follow general lab safety rules, as well as the safety procedures outlined in your risk assessment (see above).

Getting dressed standard procedure — underpants on the inside...

Don't just identify the risks in your risk assessment — you need say how to reduce or avoid them too.

Unit 3 — Controlled Assessment   ** He's actually carrying a rare bird's egg in his hat — if this fell, it could ruin someone's jacket.*

Standard Procedures

3) Make and Record Observations

1) You'll be told what data to collect in the standard procedure.
2) Record your observations using diagrams and tables. You might need to draw a suitable table for your data or you might be given one to use.
3) Make sure your tables are neat, and can be easily read.
4) Remember to include the units.

Example: Results for culturing bacteria.

Colony	Area of colony (mm^2)
A	16
B	4
C	9
D	6

Total number of colonies = 4

4) Make Sure Observations are Accurate

1) Measure very carefully to the units given in the standard procedure — always double-check measurements.
2) When you measure something, use the most accurate piece of equipment available.

Example: Culturing bacteria.

1) To measure 1 cm^3 of culture solution, you would use a 1 cm^3 pipette — not a conical flask.
2) To measure the area of bacterial colonies to the nearest mm^2, you would use graph paper with mm squares — not cm squares.

5) Process The Data You Collect

Once you've collected your data, you need to process it — this means doing something to the data so it's easier to see patterns in it.

1) This might involve doing a calculation with your results — you will be told what calculation you're expected to do in the standard procedure. Remember to include units if you need to.

> E.g. "6) Find the average area of the colonies produced."
> (area of A + area of B + area of C + area of D) ÷ 4 = (16 + 4 + 9 + 6) ÷ 4 = 35 ÷ 4 = <u>8.75</u> mm^2

2) You might need to show your data in a graph or a chart (p.96) — you may be told which type to use.

6) Evaluate How You Managed Risks

Finally, once all that is done, you need to write an evaluation of the way in which risks were managed. You need to think about how they were managed before, during and after the experiment.

Example: Evaluating risk management for culturing bacteria.

Before

The bottle of culture solution was checked to see if it had any hazard warning signs on it, however no warning signs were found. A risk assessment was done.

During

The risk assessment and lab safety rules were followed during the experiment. No incidents took place, so this showed that any possible risks were managed well using the risk assessment.

After

Cultures were disposed of safely, equipment was sterilised and put away, and hands were washed.

You'll have room to go into more detail in your own evaluation.

Well, I think this was all fairly standard...

In the exam, you'll get some marks for writing a risk assessment — but you'll get the top marks for writing a critical evaluation of how you managed the risks. This means you should point out the good and bad points — don't be afraid to pick holes in your risk assessment and say how you'd change it if you did the experiment again.

Unit 3 — Controlled Assessment

Suitability Tests

Believe it or not, suitability tests help you find out how suitable something is for a certain job. You have to do <u>one</u> of these too, so listen up.

Suitability Tests Can be Used to Find the Best Material...

Suitability tests can be used to <u>compare</u> the <u>properties</u> of <u>at least two</u> materials or substances, to see which is best for a particular job.

> E.g. a sports equipment designer wants to know the most suitable material to construct a diving board from. A suitability test can be used to compare different materials.

1) First, decide the <u>materials</u> to test, e.g. aluminium and wood.
2) Then describe the <u>properties</u> to test, e.g. flexibility and durability of the material.
3) Devise a suitable approach — write a <u>method</u> for an experiment that will <u>test</u> the relevant properties.
4) Complete a <u>risk assessment</u> — see page 92.
5) Carry out the tests, collecting some <u>data</u> along the way. <u>Process</u> this data and <u>analyse</u> it.
6) <u>Evaluate</u> the testing procedures used — think what could be <u>improved</u> if you did the test again.
7) Draw <u>conclusions</u> on the <u>suitability</u> of the materials — use the <u>data</u> you collected and your <u>own scientific knowledge</u> to decide which of the materials is <u>best suited</u> to the job.

...Or the Best Procedure to Use...

Suitability tests can also be used to determine the best procedure to use.

> E.g. an environmental scientist wants to know the best method for measuring pH. A suitability test can be used to compare the different procedures.

1) The first thing is to figure out <u>what procedures</u> could be used, e.g. an indicator or a pH meter.
2) Next you need to describe what the procedure <u>has to be able to do</u>, e.g. to quickly and accurately identify the pH of a substance.
3) Then write a <u>method</u> for an experiment that will test the <u>effectiveness</u> of the procedures.
4) Complete a <u>risk assessment</u>.
5) Do the experiment and <u>record the results</u>. <u>Process</u> and <u>analyse</u> the data.
6) <u>Evaluate</u> how you went about testing each procedure.
7) Draw <u>conclusions</u> on the <u>suitability</u> of the procedures.

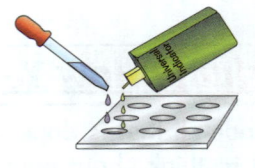

...Or the Best Equipment to Use for a Job

> E.g. a beer maker wants to determine the best device for malting barley.

1) Decide on the different <u>devices</u> to test.
2) Describe the relevant <u>properties</u> of the device, e.g. the <u>quality</u> of malted barley it produces.
3) Write a <u>method</u> for an experiment that will test the <u>effectiveness</u> of the device.
4) Complete a <u>risk assessment</u>.
5) Then carry out the method and collect some <u>data</u>. <u>Process</u> and <u>analyse</u> the data.
6) <u>Evaluate</u> the test procedure.
7) Draw <u>conclusions</u> on the <u>suitability</u> of the devices.

I wish I'd known about suitability tests before getting married...

All suitability tests are <u>quite similar</u>. They always involve deciding on <u>desirable properties</u> — you'll need to think long and hard about what you want your material/method/equipment <u>to be able to do</u>.

Unit 3 — Controlled Assessment

Suitability Tests

The suitability test is worth lots of juicy marks — so you better exactly know how they're done.

The First Step is to Describe the Purpose of the Test

The purpose of the test is basically the reason why you're carrying out the test.
1) State what's being tested and why it's being tested.
2) Describe the use or purpose of the material, procedure or device to be tested.
3) Explain how the material, procedure, or device is important in the workplace.

You'll need to do some internet research for this bit, but remember to acknowledge any sources you use (p.99).

Example: Comparing different growth media. The purpose of this suitability test is to compare three different growth media (soil, peat-based compost, and peat-free compost) to see which is the most suitable for seed germination. Growth media contain water and dissolved nutrients needed for seed germination and plant growth. They are used in the agricultural industry to germinate and grow important food crops. The type of growth medium can influence the germination rate and yield of crops.

You Need to Determine the Suitable Properties

Properties will differ from test to test but you should include things like...
1) The desirable properties or characteristics of the material, procedure or device to be tested.
2) Why these properties are important.

Example continued. The most suitable growth medium will be the one that produces the fastest germination rates. This is important in the agricultural industry to increase productivity and profits.

Write a Method That Will Test the Properties

Again the method will vary depending on what is being tested but in general you should:
1) Think about how you will make the test fair and reliable.
2) Choose suitable equipment to measure the properties.
3) Decide what observations and measurements you will record and think about how you'll record your observations. Make sure these observations and measurements link to the purpose of the test.
4) Write a step-by-step plan for your test, describing exactly what you'll do.

Example continued.
1) Fill ten pots with 100 cm^3 of soil, ten pots with 100 cm^3 peat-based compost, and ten pots with 100 cm^3 of peat-free compost.
2) Plant a barley seed in the centre of each pot, to a depth of exactly 10 mm (measured using a ruler with mm graduations).
3) Add 5 cm^3 of water to each pot.
4) Check the pots every day and record when the seedlings appear.

Your plan should be well organised, easy to follow and include scientific terms.

Assess Any Risks For Collecting Data

You'll need to do a risk assessment for the collection of your data — see page 92.

Example continued. This standard procedure is low risk. There are not many hazards involved. By following normal lab safety rules and my risk assessment, there should be no problems.

Hazard	Risk involved	How to reduce risk	In case of an accident
Bacteria in soil	Contamination of people or environment with bacteria.	Avoid hand to mouth/eye contact. Wear protective clothing. Wash hands after experiment.	Tell a teacher. Clean up any spilt soil.

Unit 3 — Controlled Assessment

Suitability Tests

Once you've planned it then you can finally get on with the test.
But it's important that you know how to record your results properly.

Use Tables to Collect and Record Data

The easiest way to record data during an experiment is usually by using a table.

1) Think about what data you are going to record and draw the table before you start.
2) Try to come up with your own table — the more independence you show, the better.
3) You should include columns or rows for any calculations as well as the data you're going to collect.
4) Label your table clearly, showing what you are measuring and what units you've used.

Example continued.

Growth media	Soil	Peat-based compost	Peat-free compost
	9	3	5
	10	4	6
	8	3	4
	9	5	6
Number of days for germination	9	4	6
	7	3	5
	10	3	4
	8	4	7
	9	5	4
	8	5	4
Average	8.7	3.9	5.1

Collect a Range of Data That is Precise and Reliable

1) Collect plenty of data — enough to make sure that the results are reliable (repeatable and reproducible).
2) Make sure your range of measurements is broad enough, e.g. if you're collecting data at different temperatures, choosing 10, 20, 30, 40 and 50 °C would be better than 10, 11, 12, 13 and 14 °C.
3) You should repeat measurements at least three times — this improves reliability.
4) Repeat any results that don't seem right — these are called anomalous results.
5) Take averages of repeated data (ignoring anomalous results).
6) When you measure something, use the most accurate piece of equipment you can (see p.93).
7) Measure very carefully, and always double-check your measurements.

Use Diagrams to Display Your Data

There are a few different ways you can present your data — the one you use depends on what you've measured.

1) Bar charts and histograms can be used to present data in different categories.
2) Pictograms are a visually appealing type of graph — they're like bar charts but with pictures instead of bars.
3) Pie charts can be used to present data as a proportion of a whole (e.g. percentages).
4) Scatter plots show the relationship between variables.
5) If you draw a graph make sure you choose a suitable scale. You should draw a line of best fit on scatter plots.
6) You can use other diagrams such as radar charts, bubble charts and sketches — you could even include photographs.
7) Make sure you plot your data carefully.
8) Remember to include a title and labels too.

Example continued.

How growth media affect germination rate.

Use tables to record data and for eating off...

It's really important to collect a good set of data and to present it properly. Make sure you choose the right kind of graph or chart to present your data and remember to include things like a title and labels for your axes.

Unit 3 — Controlled Assessment

Suitability Tests

Once you've drawn a lovely graph or chart to show your data, the next step is to analyse the results...

You Need to Analyse and Interpret Your Results

1) Describe all the trends and patterns your results show.
   If possible, back these up with quantitative data (accurate numbers) from your results.
2) Identify any anomalous results (see previous page) and explain how you know they are anomalous results.
3) Have a look back at what you wrote about the purpose of your suitability test and the properties that would make something suitable.
4) Explain what your results tell you about the suitability of the material, method or equipment.
5) You should also think about the level of uncertainty of the results — you can't be 100% sure they're right. This is because it's tricky to measure some things to a really high level of accuracy and errors can be made when taking measurements. So you need to give a sensible range of values in which the true value could lie.

> **Example continued.** The seeds were only checked once a day and there's no way of knowing at what point a seed germinated between checks. So a seed that was recorded as having germinated at 9 days could have actually germinated at, say, 8.3 days — but you just don't know. There's a level of uncertainty in the results.

Evaluations — Describe How You Could Improve the Test

1) Discuss the quality of your data. This includes how reliable (repeatable and reproducible) it is, how accurate it is and the level of uncertainty in it.
2) Comment on things like the appropriateness of the method and the equipment.
3) Describe any problems you encountered during the test, e.g. with the apparatus or method.
4) Suggest any improvements that could be made if you carried out the test again.

> **Example continued.** The results seem to be fairly reliable. There were no anomalous results and the range of results for each growth media was quite small, suggesting that the results are reproducible. The seeds were checked once a day. Checking them three times a day could reduce the level of uncertainty.
>
> The test was easy to do, the equipment was suitable, and useful data was obtained. The test took a long time to complete, and could be improved by making the seeds germinate faster (e.g. by keeping them all at a constant, warm temperature). The test could also be improved by testing more types of growth media and by measuring the seedlings after germination to get data on growth rates.

The Last Step is to Make a Conclusion about Suitability

Finally you need to draw a conclusion about the suitability of each material, procedure or device. You should:

1) Back up your conclusion with evidence — use the data you have collected and your own scientific knowledge. Don't forget to link your ideas to the purpose of the test.
2) Discuss any limitations of the test and of your results, e.g. what your results can't tell you.
3) Discuss how these limitations affect your conclusion.

> **Example continued.** The peat-based compost had the fastest germination time at 3.9 days. This was 1.2 days quicker than for peat-free compost. So the peat-based compost would be the most suitable for seed germination from the three growth media tested. However, the suitability test only examined three different growth media. There may be other growth media that are even more suitable.

I like experimentation — draw your own conclusions...

Your suitability test report will also get marked on the quality of your scientific communication. Ya wot? In English this just means — use scientific words correctly and present all your information in a clear and well organised way. You also need to make sure that all your spelling, punctuation and grammar are spot on.

Unit 3 — Controlled Assessment

Work-related Report

The third and final thing you have to do for this module is produce a work-related report. This means looking at the application of science in the real world. The next four pages contain loads of advice that'll be dead useful when you do your report.

You Should Choose an Area of Work That Interests You

You'll find it easier and maybe even enjoyable if you choose a workplace that interests you. There are literally hundreds to choose from... health services, environmental protection, forensics, farming and broadcasting are just a few examples. No matter what it is you choose your report will involve:

1) Researching a workplace that applies science.
2) Describing the work that is carried out, and the people who do it.
3) Describing the impact regulations have on the work.
4) Describing the effect the work has on society.
5) Explaining some of the science behind the work.
6) Producing a report of your findings.

If you're into farming then you could research farming.

You Should Collect Information from a Variety of Sources

You should start working on your report by collecting plenty of information from a variety of sources. You'll need both secondary data (collected by someone else) and primary data (that you collect yourself).

1) Firstly sit down and think about where you'll find relevant information.
2) Good sources of secondary data are the internet and libraries. Also, look at careers information like job descriptions to get an idea of required skills. Professional and regulatory bodies can also be good sources of information.
3) To collect your primary data you need to get some information directly from somebody working in your chosen field. This might include asking questions face-to-face, by telephone, letter or e-mail. If possible, try and speak to more than one person.
4) One of the things you'll be assessed on is how well you select relevant information — it's really important to choose your information sources carefully.
5) It's also worth writing down where you got your information from — you'll need to acknowledge your sources properly (see p.99) to get the top marks.
6) In your report, you should discuss how valid your sources of information are — e.g. you could explain how the experience of someone you've interviewed makes them well qualified to answer your questions.
7) When I was a lad, I always wanted to be a football physiotherapist...

> **Example:** The work of a physiotherapist at a football club.
> 1) Contact a few football clubs — try writing letters to local and national clubs. Try to ask questions that give an insight into the job and find out information that you might not be able to get from books.
> 2) You could also contact physiotherapists at local hospitals who might also work with footballers.
> 3) Use the internet and libraries to gather general information on sports physiotherapy.
> 4) Visit your school's careers library and find out what kind of skills and qualifications someone hoping to be a physiotherapist should have.
> 5) Look back over other work you've done in Additional Applied Science and link the work of physiotherapists back to that.
> 6) Contact organisations such as the 'Chartered Society of Physiotherapy' and the 'Association of Chartered Physiotherapists in Sports Medicine'.

Your information could come from brown sauce or even tomato...

If you pick something that you really like or quite fancy doing when you're older then writing this report might even be mildly enjoyable. Plus you'll be picking up skills like collecting information from different sources and writing reports that'll be useful in whatever career you choose to follow. Excited? I am.

Unit 3 — Controlled Assessment

Work-related Report

Your report will contain a big description, but first there's the unpleasant subject of acknowledgements...

You Need to Acknowledge Your Sources

Put quotations and extracts from texts in quotation marks and state where they are from in brackets.

1) For example, a quotation from a book should be acknowledged like this: *author*, *page number*

   "The risk of a player picking up an injury increases with age" (Caldwell, 2004: 24)

   year the book was published

2) A quotation from a person would be acknowledged like this:

   A football club's assistant sports physiotherapist said, "I mostly work in the club treatment room." (Hughes)

3) A quotation from a website would be acknowledged like this:

   "Sports physiotherapists administer treatments that aid an athlete's performance" (www.physiocareers.org.uk)

4) At the end of your report you should write a list with the heading 'acknowledgements' or 'references'.
5) This list should contain full, detailed information about all of the sources you've used.
6) Separate the books, websites and direct quotations that you've used into different sections.
7) For books write the author(s), title, publisher and date the book was published.
   Your list should be in alphabetical order by the author's last name.
8) For websites you need to write the full web page address. Put down the date you visited the website too.
9) For quotations write the person's name, job title, place of work, the date you got the quotation and how you got it, e.g. by interview. Again, if there are several, list the people in alphabetical order by name.

Example continued.

Books
Caldwell, I. (2004) *Football, a Physio's Perspective*, Ladyburn and Myres.

Websites
http://www.physiocareers.org.uk/jobprofile.htm (viewed May 2012)

Direct quotations
John Hughes, Assistant Sports Physiotherapist, CGP FC,
(face-to-face interview on 25th May 2012)

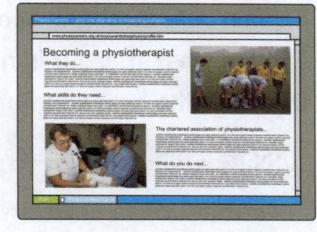

The internet can be a great source of information — but make sure you acknowledge it properly.

You Should Include a Description of the Workplace

The focus of your report should be a good description of your chosen workplace.
You should describe:

1) The structure of the organisation or workplace.
2) What type of work goes on in the organisation, the range of people that are employed and the tasks that are undertaken.
3) The purpose of your chosen job, the importance of the role and its place in the wider organisation.
4) The factors that influence the location of the workplace and how that affects or impacts society.

Example continued.

1) Describe the structure of the club (how many people work there, who is in overall charge, etc.)
2) Describe the different jobs in the club (such as managers, coaches, players, physiotherapists, etc.) and the duties, roles, responsibilities, hours of work, and tasks commonly undertaken by each.
3) Describe the purpose and importance of the physiotherapists' role (e.g. they help to keep the players fit) and how they work with other employees such as the masseurs and club doctor.
4) Explain why the workplace is located where it is (e.g. located close to a town with good road links for easy access) and the effect of this on society (e.g. provides jobs for the local community).

Unit 3 — Controlled Assessment

Work-related Report

So far, so good, but here's where it might get a little more tricky...

Describe the Qualifications and Personal Qualities Needed

For this part of your report you need to look at workers within your chosen workplace. You can get information like this from workers themselves and their job descriptions.

1) Describe the expertise of your chosen workers.
2) Explain what qualifications are required to do the job.
3) List the personal qualities needed.
4) Explain how the qualifications and qualities are relevant to the job.

Example continued.

Physiotherapists need lots of important personal qualities to carry out their job successfully. For example, they need to be a good listener to understand how an injury came about and the type of pain suffered, and should be able to explain things in a clear and calm manner. They should also care about the wellbeing of sports people, be patient and have good organisational skills.

To become a physiotherapist you need to have a relevant degree in physiotherapy, as sports physiotherapists need to have a good knowledge of the human body and the techniques they may have to use.

Include Examples of Technical Skills Used

You need to describe and explain the technical skills used in your chosen workplace.

1) Explain why and how each technical skill is used.
2) Explain what training is needed to acquire each skill.
3) Describe the procedures involved or any equipment used.

Example continued.

1) Describe a pitch-side first aid technique such as taping — strapping up an injury.
2) Describe a treatment such as massage or acupuncture.
3) Describe the use of ultrasound, electrotherapy or hydrotherapy.

Never underestimate the power of the magic sponge.

You Should Describe the Science Behind the Work

1) You should make links between the work that you've described and scientific knowledge from other modules.
2) Describe the scientific knowledge that's needed for the work.
3) Explain why scientific knowledge is important to the work described.

Example continued.

Physiotherapists need a good understanding of human biology and the effects of exercise. They also need an understanding of common sports injuries and how to prevent, identify and treat them. This is so they can assess an injury and what caused it, and so they can decide on the best treatment and rehabilitation programme.

For example, they must know the structure of the knee (a joint) and the common symptoms for injuries to the various parts of the knee. By assessing the injury and using their scientific knowledge, the physiotherapist can decide which part of the knee is injured and give the correct treatment for that specific injury.

Knowledge of thirst aid treatments, water = good...

Remember, if you want to get those big marks then describing the scientific knowledge needed by your chosen worker is an absolute must. Make sure you clearly explain how they use this knowledge in their role too.

Unit 3 — Controlled Assessment

Work-related Report

Gosh, it turns out there's rather a lot to this work-related report lark. Luckily this is the last page — all that's left to do is think about some regulatory and financial factors that affect your chosen work. And then how the devil you're going to present it all.

Discuss the Impact of Regulatory or Financial Factors

Your report should include at least two examples of financial or regulatory factors that affect the work. These can include things like health and safety legislation, chartered societies and associations.

> **Example continued.**
>
> Financial factors will affect the employment of physiotherapists. Large clubs that have a large income can afford physiotherapy centres, with multiple physiotherapists and treatment areas. Smaller clubs may not have their own physiotherapist. So, players at larger clubs may have shorter injury recovery times than those at smaller clubs.
>
> Physiotherapists must register with the Health Professions Council (HPC) if they wish to work within the NHS. This gives reassurance for patients that the physiotherapist is fully qualified. The HPC demands that physiotherapists must meet certain standards — it can stop a physiotherapist from doing their job if they don't meet these standards.

You Could Use Visual Aids to Show Information

Pictures, charts and diagrams can be used in your report to display relevant information — and to make it look pretty.

1) Data can be displayed in tables, graphs and charts (see p.96 for more on the different types).
2) You can use sketches or photographs to illustrate important information.
3) Make sure all your visual aids have titles and labels where needed.

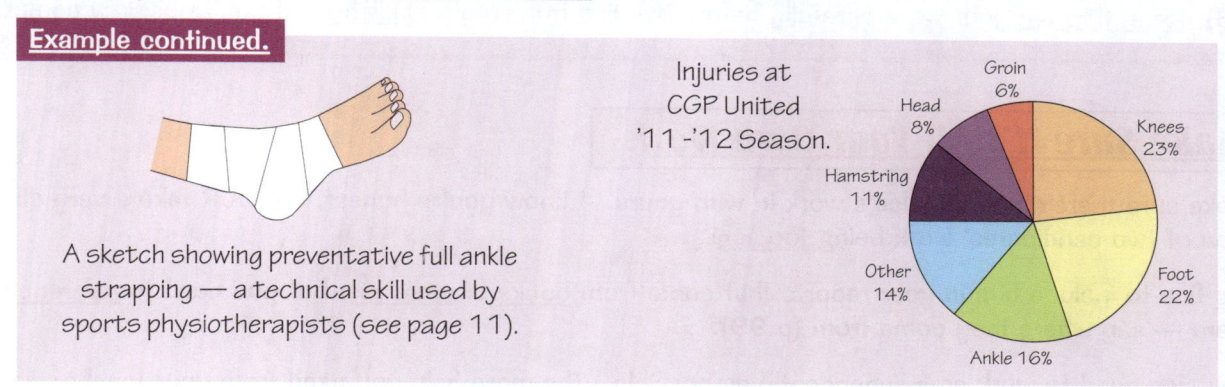

> **Example continued.**
>
> A sketch showing preventative full ankle strapping — a technical skill used by sports physiotherapists (see page 11).
>
> Injuries at CGP United '11 -'12 Season.
> - Groin 6%
> - Head 8%
> - Knees 23%
> - Hamstring 11%
> - Foot 22%
> - Other 14%
> - Ankle 16%

Make Sure Your Report is Well Organised

1) Make sure your report has a clear structure with headings for the different sections.
2) Use page numbering and include a contents page with the page number of each section.
3) Include an acknowledgements page at the end of the report (see page 99).
4) When you've finished, double-check that everything makes sense and reads well.
5) Take care with spelling and punctuation — do a spelling and grammar check.

My mam has visual aids — she calls them glasses...

Phew, that's over. Hopefully the last few pages have given you some ideas about what to include in your work-related report. It might also give you an insight into how the things you learn in class are applied in the real world.

Unit 3 — Controlled Assessment

Report Writing Advice

Even if you think this stuff is blindingly obvious, READ IT anyway — humour me.
It's a list of the stuff you must remember when you're putting your reports together...

You'll Need to Produce Two Reports

1) Remember standard procedures way back on pages 92-93 — you'll have to be able to follow four standard procedures. Luckily you don't have to write a report on these.
2) But, you will have to write one report about a suitability test (pages 94-97) and another one on a chosen area of work (pages 98-101).
3) The reports will be marked by your teacher and moderated by OCR.
4) Following standard procedures and writing two reports makes up 60% of your final mark.

I'm not impressed

Your Reports Should be Neat and Easy to Follow

If you hand in a jumbled, illegible mess and call it a portfolio, your teacher will NOT be impressed.

1) Your reports should be well organised, well structured and tailored to the tasks (so no random notes from lessons, no unidentified graphs or diagrams, no pictures of Elvis).
2) If you've got access to a computer, word process your reports — they're much neater that way, and it's easier to edit your work if you change your mind about something.
3) Make life easy for your marker — break up your report with headings to make it easier to follow.
4) If you're including any graphs, diagrams or photos, make sure they're clearly labelled.
5) There's no right or wrong length for a report. But they should be only as long as they need to be to cover everything. Don't pad them out for the sake of it — no one likes wading through waffle.
6) Read through your work carefully before handing it in (run a spellcheck if you're using a computer).

Make Sure It's All Your Own Work

Make sure there's nobody else's work in with yours. I know you're honest, but OCR take a very dim view of two candidates' work being too similar.

It's fine to include bits in your reports that come from books or websites, but you need to reference them — say where they come from (p.99).

You also need to work as independently as possible. The more help you need from your teacher, the lower your mark. But, saying that, it's better to do something with help than just miss it out altogether.

And Then for a Few Finishing Touches

Clear presentation makes your report easier to follow... which makes life easier for the person marking it... which puts them in a good mood... which has got to be good. Here are a few tricks:

1) Make a front cover for your report. It should have your name, the course name and the unit number and title. (There's an official cover sheet to go in front of this as well — ask your teacher.)
2) Number your pages. Call the first page "page 1", then just number through to the end.
3) Include a contents page with page numbers.
4) Hole-punch everything and put it in a ring binder... and you're done. Woohoo!

Unit 3 — Controlled Assessment

The Perfect Cup of Tea

The making and drinking of tea are important life skills. It's not something that will crop up in the exam, but it is something that will make your revision much easier. So here's a guide to making the perfect cuppa...

1) Choose the Right Mug

A good mug is an essential part of the tea drinking experience, but choosing the right vessel for your tea can be tricky. Here's a guide to choosing your mug:

Some bad mugs:
- No handles.
- Too fancy (and saucers are for grannies).
- Too flimsy and too 80s.
- Too many handles.

The perfect mug:
- Holds just the right amount of tea.
- Wide enough to dunk a biscuit.
- Has a design that complements your personality (yes, I'm a bit hippy).
- Nice, easy to hold handle.

2) Get Some Water and Boil It

For a really great brew follow these easy step-by-step instructions:

1) First, pour some water into a kettle and switch it on. (Check it's switched on at the wall too.)
2) Let the kettle boil. While you're waiting, see what's on TV later and check your belly button for fluff. Oh, and put a tea bag in a mug.
3) Once the kettle has boiled, pour the water into the mug.
4) Mash the tea bag about a bit with a spoon. Remove the tea bag.
5) Add a splash of milk (and a lump of sugar or two if you're feeling naughty).

Top tea tip no. 23: why not ask your mum if she wants a cup too?

Note: some people may tell you to add the milk before the tea. Scientists have recently confirmed that this is nonsense.

3) Sit Back and Relax

Now this is important — once you've made your cuppa:

1) Have a quick rummage in the kitchen cupboards for a cheeky biscuit. (Custard creams are best — steer clear of any ginger biscuits — they're evil.)
2) Find your favourite armchair/beanbag. Move the cat.
3) Sit back and enjoy your mug of tea. You've earned it.

Phew — time for a brew I reckon...

It's best to ignore what other people say about making cups of tea and follow this method. Trust me, this is the most definitive and effective method. If you don't do it this way, you'll have a shoddy drinking experience. There, you've been warned. Now go and get the kettle on. Mine's milk and two sugars...

Index

A

absorbing surfaces 54
Accident and Emergency (A and E) departments 18
accreditation (public laboratories) 27
accuracy 27, 93
acids 30, 78-80
acknowledging sources 99
acoustic ceiling tiles 54
acoustic properties 53
aerobic exercises 10
aerobic fitness 2, 4
aerobic respiration 7
aerobic respiration (in yeast) 68
agriculture 58, 59
alkalis 30, 78
alveoli 5
ammonia 77, 78
amnion 20
amniotic fluid 20
amplifiers 55
amplitude 53
anabolic steroids 10
anaemia 23
anaerobic fermentation (in bacteria) 69
anaerobic respiration 7
anaerobic respiration (in yeast) 68
angle of incidence 50
angle of reflection 50
animal growth (factors affecting) 64
animal welfare 59
anomalous results 96
antenatal care 22
aperture 52
APGAR scale 24
arable farming 58
arteries 6
artificial fertilisers 61
artificial insemination (AI) 65
aseptic techniques 67
atria 7

B

babies 24
baseline assessments 2-4
bases 78
batch cultures 70
bioreactors 71
biotechnology 58, 67-72
blood 6
blood pressure 3, 22
blood tests 23
blue light 49
body mass index (BMI) 4
bones 9
bread wheat 62
breathing system 5
British Standards Institution (BSI) 41
brittleness (of materials) 42
bronchi 5
bronchioles 5
BSI Kitemark 41
bulk chemicals 77
bullets under a microscope 37
burettes 85

C

calculating
  areas 29
  body mass index (BMI) 4
  chemical yields 86
  crop yields 63
  dry mass 63
  fertiliser applications 63
  germination rates 63
  magnifying power 36
  population growth of microorganisms 70
  rates of reaction 87
  R_f values 35
  speed 10
  the energy stored in a stretched sample 43
calibration graphs 34
cameras 52
capillaries 6
carbon dioxide 6, 7, 68
cartilage 9
catalysts 88
cattle 64, 65
CE mark 41
ceramics 45
cervix 20
chain of food production 59
cheese 69
chemical engineers 74
chemical formulae 80
chemical industries 74, 75
chemical plant managers 74
chemical production 77
chemical synthesis 86
chromatograms 35
chromatography 35
chymosin 69, 72
circuits (electrical) 55
climate change 28
coaches 1
coffee 69
collecting data 98
collecting samples 28
colorimetry 34
communication skills 12
comparing images 29
composites 46
compression 42
compressive strength 42
concentrations 81
conclusions 97
concrete 46
consent 19
consumer protection 90
contamination (in food production) 67
continuous cultures 70
contrast 29
controlled assessment 92-102
controlling sound 54
converging lenses 51, 52
copper 77
counselling (for IVF) 21
crop yields 61, 63
crystallisation 84

D

dairy farming 58, 64, 65
decibel (dB) scale 53
density (of materials) 42
dentists 15
depth of field 29
designing sports equipment 41
development tests 24
diabetes 22
diagnostic procedures 19
diaphragm 5
dimmers (in circuits) 55
dissolved solids 31
diuretics 10
diverging lenses 51
DNA databases 39
DNA profiling 39
doctors 15
double-glazing 54
Down's syndrome 23
drawings (schematic) 56
drugs 10
dry mass 63
durability 42
durum wheat 62
dyes 77

Index

E

ears 53
electrical circuits 55
electron micrographs 36, 37
electrophoresis 39
emergency care 18
emergency exits 56
emergency lighting 56
emulsions 89
enforcement officers 60
Environment Agency 26
environmental health officers 60
environmental protection officers 26
enzymes (in food production) 69, 72
European Committee for Standardisation 41
evacuation times 56
evaluations 93, 97
evaporation 84
exhaling 5
exponential growth 70
eyepiece lenses (in microscopes) 36

F

factory inspectors 60
fallopian tubes 20
Farmer Giles 64
feedback 55
female reproductive system 20
fermentation 68
fertilisation 20, 21
fertilisers 61, 63, 77
fertility clinics 19
fibreglass 46
fibres (under a microscope) 38
filters 49
filtration 83, 84
financial factors 101
fine chemicals 77
fingerprints 38
fireproof curtains 56
fireproof doors 56
fitness 2
fitness facilities 1
fitness practitioners 1, 12
flexibility (of materials) 42
fluid-filled dampers 54
fluorescent lamps 49
focal plane (in a camera) 52
Food Standards Agency 33

food
  additives 72
  colourings 72
  poisoning 67
  production (chain of) 59
  quality and safety 60
  safety legislation 33
  spoilage 67
  technologists 60
footprints 29
force-extension graphs 43
Forensic Science Service 33
forensic scientists 33
forgeries 35
frequency 53
fungicides 61

G

General Practitioners (GPs) 19
genetically modified (GM) organisms 72
germination rates 63
gestational diabetes 22
glucose 6, 7
golf balls 46
good laboratory practice 27
graphs and tables 96
green light 49
growth charts 24

H

hairs (under a microscope) 38
hardness (of materials) 42
hazchem symbols 76
health (definition) 2
Health and Safety Executive (HSE) 75
health and safety regulations 1, 15, 26, 48, 59, 75
health and safety (venues) 56
health care organisations 14
health care practitioners 15
health centres 14
health education 16
Health Protection Agency 67
health visitors 24
hearing loss 53
heart 7
heat (sources of) 56
herbicides 61
hertz (Hz) 53
high blood pressure in pregnancy 22
hospitals 14
howl 55

I

implantation 20
incandescent lamps 49
indicator organisms 28
indoor venues 56
informed consent 19
infra-red (IR) radiation 49
inhaling 5
inorganic farming 61
insecticides 61
insoluble salts 82, 83
intercostal muscles 5
International Organisation for Standards (ISO) 41
iron 77
isolating vibrations 54
IVF (*in vitro* fertilisation) 21

J

joints 9

K

KEVLAR® 46
kidneys 8

L

lab technicians 33, 74
lactic acid 6, 7, 69
Lactobaccili 69
lag phase 70
lasers 49
law of reflection 50
lenses 51, 52
lifestyle (definition) 2
lifestyle improvements 16
ligaments 9
light engineers 48
light microscopes 36
   interpreting images from 37
light (optical) properties 50
light sources 49
lighting effects 48-52
litmus paper 30
loudness 53
loudspeakers 55
lungs 5

Index

M

magnification 29, 36
magnifying power 36
managing indoor venues 56
material properties 45, 46
material scientists 41
mayfly larvae 28
measuring objects 29
measuring turbidity 31
mechanical properties 42
medical history 17
medical treatments 16, 18, 19
metal
  carbonates 80
  extraction 77
  hydroxides 79
  oxides 79
metals 45
microorganisms 67-72
microorganisms (growth of) 70
microphones 55
microscopes 36-38
midwives 22, 24
milk 66
mirrors 50
mixtures 89
muscle-building exercises 10
muscles 9
music venues 54-56
mycoprotein 68

N

National Health Service (NHS) 14
neutralisation reactions 78, 85
nurses 15
nutritionists 15

O

objective lenses (in microscopes) 36
opaque materials 50
operations 16
optical properties 50
opticians 15
organic farming 61
oxygen 6, 7, 68

P

paper chromatography 35
parallel circuits 55
paramedics 18
pasteurisation 66
pathogens 67
percentage yields 86
percentiles on growth charts 24
performance-enhancing drugs 10
performance venues 56
permanent records 29
personal trainers 1
pesticides 61
pH 30, 78
pH meters 30
pharmacists 15
physiotherapists 11
pigments 77
pitch 53
placenta 20
plane mirrors 50
plasma 6
platelets 6
pollen (under a microscope) 37
polymers 45
post-natal care 24
post-treatment survival times 16
precipitation reactions 82
precise results 27
pre-eclampsia 22
pregnancy 20-23
presenting data 96
primary data 98
prioritising treatment 18
processing data 93
proficiency tests 27
public analysts 33
public health 16
pulse rate 3

Q

qualitative tests 30
quality assurance 90
quantitative tests 30

R

radiation 49
rates of reaction 87, 88
rat-tailed maggots 28
raw materials 78
ray diagrams (converging lenses) 52
ray diagrams (plane mirrors) 50
recording data 93, 96
red blood cells 6
red light 49
reference samples 37
reference solutions 34
referencing sources 99
referrals (from GPs) 19
reflective materials 50
reflective surfaces 54
refraction 50, 51
regulations
  for environmental protection officers 26
  for fitness practitioners 1
  for health care practitioners 15
  in agriculture 59
  in performance venues 56
  in stage and screen 48
  of the chemical industry 75
reliability 27, 96
removing fat (from milk) 66
report writing 102
representative samples 28
Resazurin test 66
research chemists 74
residues 83
resources (in the NHS) 18
respiration 7
R_f values 35
ribs 5
RICE method 11
risk assessments 76, 92
risks of treatments 19

S

safety margins 41
safety standards 41
salts 79, 80, 82-85
sampling the environment 28
scanning electron microscopes 36
  interpreting images from 37
scene of crime officers 33
schematic drawings 56
secondary data 98
selective breeding 65
semi-quantitative tests 30
senescence (death phase) 70
series circuits 55
sharpness of focus 29
shutter (in a camera) 52
skeletal-muscular injuries 11
sludge-worms 28
sodium hydroxide 77, 78

Index

soil conditions (for growing wheat) 61
soluble salts 84, 85
solutes 81
solutions 81
solvents 81
sound (controlling) 54
sound effects 48, 53, 54
sound engineers 48
sound systems 55
soya sauce 69
special effects 48
speciality chemicals 77
speed 10
sphygmomanometers 3
spina bifida 23
sports equipment 41
spring wheat 62
stage and screen performances 48
stamina 2
standard procedures 92, 93
stationary phase 70
steroids 10
stiffness (of materials) 42, 43
stonefly larvae 28
suitability tests 94-97
sulfuric acid 77, 78
sunlight 49
suspended solids 31
suspensions 89
switches (in circuits) 55

T

tables and graphs 96
taste testing 60
tea 103
temperature (body) 3
tendons 9
tennis racquets 46
tensile strength 42
tension 42
test kits (to monitor the environment) 30
testing formulations 90
testing techniques 30
testing water quality 31
theoretical yields 86
thermal conductivity 44
thermal insulators 44
thermal properties 44
thermal reflectivity 44
thermometers 3
thin-layer chromatography 35

tinnitus 53
titrations 85
toughness (of materials) 42
trachea 5
translucent materials 50
transparent materials 50
triage 18
triage nurses 18
turbidity 31

U

UHT milk 66
ultrasound scans 22
ultra-violet (UV) radiation 49
uncertainty (of data) 97
underlay 54
unhappy cows 29
Universal Indicator 30
urea 8
urine samples (in pregnancy) 22
urine tests (for drugs) 10
uterus 20

V

vaccinations 16
valves (in the heart) 7
valves (in veins) 6
veins 6
ventilation 56
ventricles 7
vibrations 53, 54
viewfinder (in a camera) 52
virtual images 50
visual effects 48
visual examination 29, 38
vitamins 72

W

water lice 28
water pollution 28
wheat production 61-63
wheat (types of) 62
white blood cells 6
white light 49
winter wheat 62
wooden spoons 44
work-related reports 98-101
world's fastest yoghurt 69

Y

yeast 68
yeast extract 68
yields (of chemicals) 86
yields (of milk) 64
yields (of wheat) 63
yoghurt 69

Answers

Revision Summary for Unit 1: Topic 1 (page 13)

11) BMI = body mass in kg ÷ (height in m)^2
    BMI = 85 ÷ (1.8)^2 = 85 ÷ 3.24 = 26.2

25) speed = distance ÷ time
    speed = 11 m ÷ 0.25 seconds = 44 m/s

Revision Summary for Unit 1: Topic 2 (page 25)

10) Gerald, Gareth, Angela, Susan

Revision Summary for Unit 1: Topic 4 (page 40)

9) R_f = distance travelled by substance ÷ distance travelled by solvent
   R_f = 4.5 ÷ 12 = 0.375

11) Magnifying power = eyepiece lens magnification × objective lens magnification
    a) Magnifying power = 10 × 40 = ×400
    b) Magnifying power = 8 × 25 = ×200

Revision Summary for Unit 2: Topic 1 (page 47)

9) C

17) a) B (because it's hard and strong to protect the cyclist, but lightweight so as not to slow the cyclist down).
    b) D (because it's tough, strong and durable enough to withstand being dragged across rough ground).
    c) A (because it's very light for it's strength, and for a high-performance piece of equipment you're willing to pay for it).

Revision Summary for Unit 2: Topic 3 (page 73)

13) 85% of 600 = $\frac{85}{100}$ × 600 = 510 seeds will germinate.

Revision Summary for Unit 2: Topic 4 (page 91)

14) sodium hydroxide + nitric acid → sodium nitrate + water

15) calcium carbonate + hydrochloric acid → calcium chloride + water + carbon dioxide

17) Mass = concentration × volume
    Mass = 0.5 × 600 = 300 g

24) Percentage yield = (yield ÷ theoretical yield) × 100
    Percentage yield = (40 ÷ 52) × 100 = 77%

27) 60 s